# Revisiting
# RAHAB

## ANOTHER LOOK AT
## THE WOMAN OF JERICHO

**Revisiting Rahab: Another Look at the Woman of Jericho**

The General Board of Higher Education and Ministry leads and serves The United Methodist Church in the recruitment, preparation, nurture, education, and support of Christian leaders—lay and clergy—for the work of making disciples of Jesus Christ for the transformation of the world. Its vision is that a new generation of Christian leaders will commit boldly to Jesus Christ and be characterized by intellectual excellence, moral integrity, spiritual courage, and holiness of heart and life. The General Board of Higher Education and Ministry of The United Methodist Church serves as an advocate for the intellectual life of the church. The Board's mission embodies the Wesleyan tradition of commitment to the education of laypersons and ordained persons by providing access to higher education for all persons.

Wesley's Foundery Books is named for the abandoned foundery that early followers of John Wesley transformed, which later became the cradle of London's Methodist movement.

**Revisiting Rahab: Another Look at the Woman of Jericho**

Copyright 2021 by Wesley's Foundery Books

Wesley's Foundery Books is an imprint of the General Board of Higher Education and Ministry, The United Methodist Church. All rights reserved.

No part of this book may be reproduced in any form whatsoever, print or electronic, without written permission, except in the case of brief quotations embodied in critical articles or reviews. For information regarding rights and permissions, contact the Publisher, General Board of Higher Education and Ministry, PO Box 340007, Nashville, TN 37203-0007; phone 615-340-7393; fax 615-340-7048. Visit our website at www.gbhem.org.

All web addresses were correct and operational at the time of publication.

978-1-953052-00-1

Scripture quotations, unless otherwise noted, are from New Revised Standard Version Bible, copyright © 1989 by the Division of Christian Education of the National Council of the Churches of Christ in the USA. Used by permission. All rights reserved worldwide. http://nrsvbibles.org/

Scripture quotations marked NIV are taken from the Holy Bible, New International Version®, NIV®. Copyright © 1973, 1978, 1984, 2011 by Biblica, Inc.® Used by permission of Zondervan. All rights reserved worldwide. www.zondervan.com. The "NIV" and "New International Version" are trademarks registered in the United States Patent and Trademark Office by Biblica, Inc.™

Scriptures marked KJV are from the King James Version (public domain).

Scriptures marked The Message are taken from THE MESSAGE, copyright © 1993, 2002, 2018 by Eugene H. Peterson. Used by permission of NavPress, represented by Tyndale House Publishers. All rights reserved.

Scriptures marked NEB are taken from the New English Bible, copyright © Cambridge University Press and Oxford University Press 1961, 1970. All rights reserved.

Scriptures marked NKJV are taken from the New King James Version®. Copyright © 1982 by Thomas Nelson. Used by permission. All rights reserved.

GBHEM Publishing is an affiliate member of the Association of University Presses.

Manufactured in the United States of America

**HIGHER EDUCATION & MINISTRY**
General Board of Higher Education and Ministry
THE UNITED METHODIST CHURCH

# CONTENTS

# ABBREVIATIONS

| ABD | *The Anchor Bible Dictionary*, edited by D. N. Freedman |
| BDB | F. Brown, S. R. Driver, and C. A. Briggs, *A Hebrew and English Lexicon of the Old Testament* |
| Bib | *Biblica* |
| BibInt | *Biblical Interpretation* |
| HALOT | L. Koehler, W. Baumgartner, and J. J. Stamm, *The Hebrew and Aramaic Lexicon of the Old Testament*, translated and edited under the supervision of M. E. J. Richardson; 4 volumes, 1994–1999 |
| HTR | *The Harvard Theological Review* |
| JBL | *Journal of Biblical Literature* |
| JBQ | *The Jewish Bible Quarterly* |
| JFSR | *Journal of Feminist Studies in Religion* |
| JNES | *Journal of Near Eastern Studies* |
| JSOT | *Journal for the Study of the Old Testament* |
| JSOTSup | *Journal for the Study of the Old Testament Supplement* |
| MLN | *Modern Language Notes* |
| NBD | *New Bible Dictionary* |

| | |
|---|---|
| SJT | *Scottish Journal of Theology* |
| TynBul | *Tyndale Bulletin* |
| USQR | *Union Seminary Quarterly Review* |
| VT | *Vetus Testamentum* |
| VTSup | *Vetus Testamentum Supplement* |

# ACKNOWLEDGMENTS

This work began in 2017 when I taught a two-week course at Emory University's Candler School of Theology as the visiting Sankofa scholar. I am grateful to Rev. Dr. Toni Belin Ingram and her leadership team at Candler for encouraging me to "think outside the box" and develop a new course that became *Connecting the Canons: Sacred and Secular*. The students who participated in that trial run course could not have known it, but they (and their enthusiasm) set me on a trajectory that would refine my syllabus and evolve my scholarship. The chapter "Recasting Rahab: Reading Rahab with African American Literature" grew out of that very course. A version of the chapter has previously appeared in *Horizons in Biblical Theology* (2020).

This book project began as a collection of essays. When I first shared my plan to write a book that would be a collection of essays about the biblical Rahab, not everyone was excited about the idea. A close scholar-friend was so worried about the viability of such a project that, unbeknownst to me, they spent the better part of a night researching the topic online. The next morning they happily reported there was a gap in the scholarship, I could fill the gap, and

I should proceed with my idea. Although I had already begun my work and did not necessarily need their approval to move forward with the project, I trust my scholar-friend will find many of their initial concerns are resolved in this finished product.

Because I wanted this book to be accessible for a wide variety of readers, I knew my choice of publishers was important. I acknowledge I sought out a publishing house that would be careful with my scholarship and its presentation. M. Kathryn Armistead and the publishing team at the United Methodist General Board of Higher Education and Ministry provided invaluable insight and encouragement at different stages of this project's development. I am particularly grateful to Kathy for the care she took in helping me to fine-tune my ideas and for the grace she extended regarding writing deadlines as I did my best to focus in the midst of a global pandemic and the death of my father toward the end of the manuscript's completion.

Before the pandemic forced stay-at-home orders, I spent many days writing offsite in local coffee shops, quiet hotel lobbies, and apartment complex conference rooms. I am grateful to the professional and caring management team at The Quarry at River North (Indianapolis, IN) for their encouragement to use their common areas as my ad hoc satellite office. Whether they know it or not, at least one chapter of this book was written and edited while sipping on a hot beverage from their coffee bar as I sat beside their pool, at their conference room table, or in their private dining room.

Here, I acknowledge President David Mellott and Dean Leah Gunning Francis of Christian Theological Seminary (CTS) for their unwavering support of my scholarship and this project. President Mellott, Dean Francis, and my CTS colleagues encouraged my work inside and outside the classroom. One colleague would often pass me in the hallway and routinely offer an affirming cheer, "Let nothing separate you from your book, Russaw!" For this I am grateful. I am also thankful for my CTS students (especially those enrolled in my *Connecting the Canons* courses) who allowed me to test out ideas during our class discussions. Those members of the soon-to-be-famous(er) 150 cohort of the PhD program who enrolled in the 2020 session of the course breathed new life into this project as, through their sermonic presentations, they modeled for the entire class how the work of *Connecting* may have "legs" in our classrooms AND our pulpits.

*Revisiting Rahab* is written for an audience of seminarians, seminary-trained clergy, and inquisitive laypersons. I am thankful for clergy friends who embrace my ministry of scholar-practitioner. Bishop Sharma D. Lewis of The United Methodist Church fully engaged select portions of this book with an eye toward its usefulness in the larger church. The Rev. Dr. Valerie Toney Parker of the African Methodist Episcopal Church graciously read and provided feedback on many chapters of *Revisiting Rahab* at various stages of its development. Similarly, colleagues like Dr. Christina J. Davis (Christian Theological Seminary), Dr. Febbie C. Dickerson (American Baptist College), Dr. Alisha Lola Jones (Indiana University–Bloomington), and Dr. Chris Paris (Urshan Graduate School of Theology) each provided feedback on chapter drafts from their particular vantage points as seminary, college, and university professors. All is Wells.

Dr. Shively T. J. Smith covenanted to do work together during the pandemic. Our many FaceTime and Zoom calls encouraged this work and kept me focused in ways that I may never be able to adequately articulate. I have no doubt that her affirmations and admonishments made this work better. Shively, know that I am deeply appreciative of you, your scholarship, your friendship, and your willingness to read my work and talk about it out loud.

Finally, from beginning to end, I have benefited from the support of my family. I know my family—and friends who act like family—grew tired of me talking about Rahab. I am also convinced my father, Dr. Floyd Russaw, is proudly weaving his oldest daughter's new book title into heavenly conversation as he now enjoys his time among the ancestors.

# INTRODUCTION

## Revisiting Rahab: A Reintroduction to a Familiar Character

Rahab is an important character in the Hebrew Bible canon. Despite her non-Israelite status and questionable station in society, her words and actions facilitate the Israelites' entrance into the promised land of Canaan. Most of us are familiar with the basics. We first encounter Rahab in the book of Joshua as the Israelites are on the cusp of entering the land of promise. According to Joshua 2, the Israelites' new leader sends two men on a reconnaissance mission to assess the threat of the people of Canaan. These two men breach the walls of Jericho, enter the home of a prostitute named Rahab, and settle there. When the king's envoy asks about the whereabouts of possible foreign spies in the community, Rahab protects the two Israelite men. She hides the Israelites on her roof and sends the royal representatives on a wild goose chase. The Israelite spies return to Joshua and, based upon Rahab's testimony, report the LORD has given Canaan to them. Later, when the Israelites invade Canaan, the two men rescue Rahab and her family from destruction. The Israelite attack on Canaan is successful because of Rahab. To be clear, the story of the Israelite settlement in Canaan hinges on the character Rahab.

Despite her critical role in the macro narrative of the ancient Israelites, Rahab has been relegated to the crevices of the larger story of the Israelites and their God. Many readers do not have much to say about Rahab other than that she was the prostitute who helped the Israelite spies. In many ways, Rahab has been pushed to the edges of the imaginations of even the most creative and inquisitive readers. However, the biblical Rahab is an intriguing character whose story is layered with important concerns for modern readers. Despite—or perhaps precisely because of—her marginalized position, a careful re-read of Rahab's story prompts questions around matters of identity, autonomy, difference, and privilege.

This chapter introduces the *Revisiting Rahab* project. Here I establish the purpose of the book, rehearse the contours of Rahab's narrative, and preview the subsequent chapters. With this book I aim to retrieve Rahab from the periphery and place her at the center of a series of close readings, which I hope inform a more freeing and liberative understanding of characters found in the text and in front of the text.

Rahab is, indeed, a character worth revisiting. The biblical Rahab has been taken up in surprising parts of popular culture. For example, within the music industry the heavy metal group Earth Groans named one of their albums *Rahab*.[1] Additionally, Rahab has captured the imagination of non-fiction and fiction authors alike. Among popular literature, Liz Curtis Higgs lists Rahab among the *Bad Girls of the Bible*; Kasey van Norman frames Rahab as assertive, confident, and doing what she had to do to support her family in *Rahab: Don't Judge Me, God Says I'm Qualified* in the Known by Name series; and Jill Eileen Smith dramatizes

Rahab as the wife of a gambler who finds herself sold as a slave to cover her husband's debt and is soon forced into prostitution in *The Crimson Cord: Rahab's Story.*[2]

## Chapter Outline

With *Revisiting Rahab* I do not engage in text-critical debates such as dating and authorship. I simply work with the text in its final, canonical form. I also bracket out such interpretive niceties as the concern of the red cord. In this sense *Revisiting Rahab* extends or adds to an established general understanding of the story of Rahab. The chapter "Representing Rahab: The Language of *Zonah*" takes up Rahab's designation as a sex worker. This chapter establishes a foundational knowledge base, as the many interpretations of Rahab's story turn on her designation as a prostitute. Said differently, this designation is the common ground with which many readers of Rahab's story seem to align. It seems one cannot tell Rahab's story without referencing her occupation. Different readings of Rahab's story have attended to the linguistic nuances, literary representations, and social expectations of the Hebrew word *zonah* for many years. These readings tend to focus on the socially transgressive work of prostitution in ways that foreclose on any ability to understand Rahab as anything other than her prescribed profession. Because people focus on Rahab's story based on the prostitute label placed upon her, this chapter examines the many ways the Hebrew word *zonah* functions in the Hebrew Bible to aid modern readers in their understanding of this foundational aspect of Rahab's characterization. And so *Revisiting Rahab* begins with a treatment of the Hebrew word for prostitute.

The chapter "Researching Rahab: Major Streams of Investigation" builds upon the initial examination of Rahab's designation as a *zonah* or prostitute and extends the study to include her status as a foreign woman and her function as the unlikely hero in the story of Israel's entrance into Canaan. In this way, this chapter grounds the reader in the three major streams of scholarly inquiry around Rahab. Importantly, "Researching Rahab" does not put scholarly voices in conflict with each other or establish a hierarchy wherein certain voices are privileged or allowed to eclipse other equally valid interpretive conclusions. There are many ways to understand Rahab. Readers can and should hold these many interpretive possibilities in tension with one another.

Having established the foundational elements of Rahab's story, I turn to the work of reading her story through various interpretive lenses. The chapter "Recasting Rahab: Reading Rahab with African American Literature" is a treatment of Rahab alongside characters from Harlem Renaissance writer Nella Larsen's novels *Passing* and *Quicksand*. This chapter riffs on the basic melody of Rahab's story by juxtaposing the biblical Rahab with two Larsen characters, and positioning all three characters as engaged in the act of passing.

Relying on the tools of rhetorical criticism, the chapter "Revealing Rahab: A New Interpretive Strategy" closely examines the encounter between Rahab and the Israelite men and interrogates elements of their negotiation. Here, I take seriously the power dynamics in Rahab's interaction with the Israelite men and argue the contours of their agreement mirror a covenant or treaty in which Rahab assumes the role of the powerful suzerain and the Israelites are positioned under her authority as the vassal. This interpretive possibility may surprise readers because it challenges traditional renderings of the power dynamics between the Canaanite woman and the two Israelite men.

In the final chapter, "Reconsidering Rahab: Possibilities in the

Midst of the Israelites," I consider how Rahab navigates her perilous identity as a Canaanite woman existing on the margins of both Canaanite and Israelite society. Specifically, I attend to Rahab's identity among the Israelites after the destruction of Jericho and explore her living among the Israelites as a prisoner of war.

## How to Read This Book

Rahab is familiar to readers. Therefore, in an effort to minimize redundancy, instead of retelling her story at the beginning of each chapter, I revisit the texts associated with Rahab in this introductory chapter. Occasionally I make reference to important English translations of the Hebrew text, but for ease I rely upon the widely accessible NRSV translation in these chapters. After establishing the basic contours of Rahab's story, I also provide a brief overview of the accepted thinking associated with Rahab. Also, for consistency, unless another moniker is used in the NRSV, I will use YHWH (pronounced Yahweh) or LORD to refer to the god of the Israelites.

I recognize the story found in Joshua 6 of the destruction of Jericho is complicated by matters of authorship, transmission, literary sources and editing, and traditions. Scholarly commentaries provide great insight concerning authorship and the production of the book of Joshua, which is generally understood as a product of the Deuteronomic Historian. As such, the story contains particular ideological leanings. Two or three literary sources inform the narrative of Joshua 6.[3] Modern readers' understanding of the activity depicted in Joshua 6 is largely determined by which ancient text their English translation is drawn from. The Hebrew Masoretic text (MT) and the Greek Septuagint (LXX), do not always align. As an example, MT has Joshua call the priests and tell them to take the Ark of the Covenant and "have seven priests carry seven trumpets of rams' horns in front of the ark of the LORD" (Josh 6:6). This instruction is different in LXX, which records Joshua telling the priests to charge the people to "go round and encompass the city." There is no mention of seven priests or seven trumpets in LXX.[4] Furthermore, as with any story originally transmitted orally, tradition and cultic ritual of the community inform the editing of the narrative.[5] The theological idea of holy war and the presentation of Rahab's house being in the wall in Joshua 2 (which contradicts the presentation of the wall tumbling before she is rescued in Josh 6) complicate the story in its final form.[6] In many ways, the story is an example of an imaginative reconstruction of warfare that might have some basis in fact but without the original theological idea that the warfare was initiated and implemented by YHWH.[7]

One of the contributions of this book is how it introduces readers to the different ways of understanding Rahab. Some of these understandings will be familiar and so easily accepted by readers. Some of these approaches to Rahab and her story may be new and welcomed as refreshingly new, perhaps corrective, perspectives on a familiar text. Some approaches may pull the reader to uncomfortable spaces and lead to intense wrestling with the text. Readers may want to reject these readings outright. I welcome all of these responses in this book. In fact, one of the benefits of *Revisiting Rahab* is precisely that it might generate those many different responses from a single reader. My hope is that *Revisiting Rahab* will give its readers the tools and the permission to see and engage characters that are normally overlooked in the text and encourage them to do that in real life as well.

In each chapter I take up a different aspect of Rahab's story and offer a distinct way of reading it. Each chapter of this book can stand alone. Therefore, beyond the foundational material found in the first two chapters, readers need not read *Revisiting Rahab* in sequential order but may alight upon the topic that most interests them. However you approach this book, Rahab is a fascinating character whose story has been overlooked by many modern readers. She warrants a second look. Through these chapters, I invite you to revisit Rahab.

## Recalling Rahab's Story

After the call of Moses; the Exodus experience; the giving of the covenantal Ten Commandments; a time of wandering in the wilderness; an assurance that YHWH[8] will give the Israelites the land promised to the patriarchs Abraham, Isaac, Jacob, and their descendants; and the subsequent transfer of leadership to Joshua, the Pentateuch ends with Joshua and the Israelites positioned opposite Jericho mourning the death of Moses at Mount Nebo in Moab (Deut 34:5). As the book of Joshua opens, YHWH instructs the new military leader to lead the Israelites across the Jordan River and enter the land which YHWH is giving them (Josh 1:2). In the second chapter of the book named after him, the military leader, Joshua, sends two men to spy out the land of Canaan. The two men gain entrance into the Canaanite city of Jericho and take refuge in the home of Rahab, who is described by the biblical writer as a prostitute.

In Joshua 2:3-4 it appears that word of the Israelite spies' arrival in the city has made it to the palace, and the king of Jericho sends his official representatives to Rahab's house to inquire about the presence of foreigners in the city. When questioned about the potential threat to the Jericho community, Rahab acknowledges the foreign men indeed came to her home but explains to the king's messengers that the men have already left. Rahab claims she does not know where the foreigners have gone. In an act of treasonous misdirection, Rahab encourages the king's envoys in their pursuit of the foreigners. Rahab saves the Israelites from being discovered by the king's representatives, who certainly would have tortured and punished them as spies. Rahab then has a conversation with her guests, whom she has hidden under flax on her rooftop.

During her rooftop conversation with the Israelite men, Rahab negotiates for the safety of her family. In return for her salvific act of hospitality, the Israelite men agree to spare Rahab, her family members, and anyone else found in her home when they return to destroy Jericho. After reaching an agreement with the Israelites Rahab directs them to safety and ratifies their agreement by attaching a red cord to her window. The Israelites will use this cord to identify her home as one to not destroy when they return to invade Jericho.

Later, the Israelites invade Jericho and Joshua instructs the two who spied out the area to retrieve Rahab and her family. Rahab and all those found under her roof at the time of the Israelite invasion escape the destruction of Jericho, and the story of Rahab concludes with the surviving displaced Canaanites living among the Israelites (Josh 6:25). The Canaanite Rahab and her family survive to live out their days in the midst of the Israelites.

For many readers, Rahab's story ends in Joshua 6, but Rahab's story does not end in the book of Joshua. While no longer central to the unfolding narrative of the ancient Israelites and their god YHWH, Rahab's story continues through the Hebrew Bible, and she is even referenced in the New Testament. According to the Gospel of Matthew, the Israelite Salmon has a son named Boaz. Boaz, in turn, has a son by Ruth named Obed. Obed has a son named Jesse, and Jesse has a son named David. This David eventually becomes the king of Judah.[9] Matthew explicitly identifies Rahab as the mother of Boaz and wife of Salmon. According to the genealogy, then, Rahab is the great-great-grandmother of King David—as well as a distant matriarch of Jesus. New Testament readers are also told that Rahab is a model of faith and obedience because she "received the spies in peace" (Heb 11:31). Similarly, Rahab's works justify her, because she "welcomed the messengers and sent them out by another road" (Jas 2:25).[10]

As the mother of Obed, Rahab is a matriarch in the family of King David, and because of that relationship she occupies a significant place in the legacy of Israel. Rahab is a popular figure of modern culture and is the topic of music albums and literature. In addition to her place within the popular imagination, Rahab has captured the intellectual imagination of biblical scholars. As I complete this manuscript on the cusp of 2020, the time is right to revisit Rahab. As the nation celebrates the hundredth anniversary of the Nineteenth Amendment, which gave many women the right to vote in the United States and formally ushered in an era of women's rights that led to the feminist political movement, it is a good time to reacquaint ourselves with the woman who lived on the edge of Jericho and became an integral part of Israel's story. Moreover, in the era of #MeToo and the U. S. Supreme Court's reconsideration of *Roe v. Wade*, when controversy surrounding female bodily autonomy seems to capture news headlines weekly, now is a good time to reconsider Rahab and her story.

—— 1 ——

# REPRESENTING RAHAB
## The Language of *Zonah*

## Introduction

Rahab's description as a prostitute grounds many modern retellings of her story. This preoccupation with Rahab's prostitute status is understandable because the writer of the book of Joshua marks the character with a Hebrew term generally translated as "prostitute," "harlot," or "whore." Furthermore, the term used to describe Rahab in Joshua 2:1 appears in the three major sections of the Hebrew Bible: Torah, Prophets, and Writings. A close examination of the word and its use throughout the Hebrew canon, however, suggests these English translations may be too flat. I suspect different groups of readers understand words and phrases like "prostituting" and "playing the whore" differently based upon how they have experienced the term in other portions of the biblical text.

The ubiquitous use of the Hebrew term by the different biblical writers undoubtedly informs the impressions readers have of Rahab's character and actions. When one was called a prostitute, one was marked as contemptible, sexualized, and a threat to communities that value male honor, the confinement of sexual activities to the act of procreation, and the patriarchal control of females and their bodies. While different groups of readers living in different social contexts understand *prostitute* and *prostitution* differently, they all understand Rahab to be a prostitute.

This chapter surveys the different forms of the Hebrew terms for prostitute in order to establish a common understanding of the term that features prominently in Rahab's story. A study of any character found in the Hebrew Bible benefits from a familiarity with the Hebrew language used to describe them. In the case of Rahab, this study takes up the use of the Hebrew word for prostitute. Throughout this chapter I will introduce the Hebrew word and provide its transliteration and translation. In subsequent uses of the term it will appear in its transliterated form. I do this to remind English readers they are bridging time and culture when they read a text from the ancient Israelite context. I recognize that reading foreign words may be cumbersome for some, but my hope is this approach will expand their sense of awe for the text and world from which it most probably emerged.

The Hebrew Bible uses different forms of זֹנָה (*zonah*, "prostitute," "harlot," "whore"), to mark individuals who participate in the enterprise of prostitution or commodified sex work. Tamar impersonates a prostitute (זוֹנָה, *zonah*) in Genesis 38:15, a priest is forbidden to marry a prostitute (*zonah*) in Leviticus 21:7, and the enemies of Judah and Jerusalem trade boys for the prostitute (זוֹנָה, *zonah*) in Joel 3:3.[1] Two prostitutes (זֹנוֹת, *zonot*) seek justice from King Solomon in 1 Kings 3:16, and the prophet Ezekiel admonishes the people for their whorings (תַזְנוּת, *taznutay*) in Ezekiel 16:33. The writers of Hosea and Amos use the verb תִזְנֶינָה (*tiznenah*) to describe those who play the whore or prostitute in the city (Hos

4:13-14; Amos 7:17). Finally, the prophet Hosea is instructed to select "a wife of whoredom" (זנונים אשת, *'eshet zenunim*) in Hosea 1:2. In each of these examples, *zonah* and its various forms mark individuals who earn a living as sex workers.

Whether occurring as a singular or plural noun, a verb or an idiom, the word *zonah* is a negative marker for women in the biblical text. The word *zonah* appears most often as a noun in the Hebrew Bible and is rendered as "whore" or "prostitute" in modern English translations. *Zonah* always describes a female associated with sex work, and the association is always a shameful one. For example, Dinah's brothers seem upset when, upon learning Shechem had unauthorized sex with Dinah, they ask the question: "Should our sister be treated like a whore?" (Gen 34:31). It is because the men of the land consort with prostitutes that the daughters of the land are accused of playing the whore in Hosea 4:13-14. This situation prompts the ruin of the people. Finally, the father advises the son that the prostitute's fee is the equivalent of a meager loaf of bread in Proverbs 6:26.

I define a *zonah* as a female member of Israelite society who is held in contempt by the community because of her association with sex work, which threatens the idea that males alone control female bodies. Consequently, this chapter explores how the *zonah* designation in the Hebrew Bible in general, and in the story of Rahab in particular, prefigures Rahab for readers as one whose body is not controlled by a male. Rahab challenges the status quo by controlling her own body. Sitting with the text in modern contexts, I consider how the use of *zonah* or "prostitute" is taken up by two distinct groups of modern readers when they consider the story of Rahab. Here, I rely upon data compiled during a gathering of African American churchwomen and material from a study of the text done by contemporary sex workers and their advocates. I then turn to examine the technical vocabulary associated with *zonah* and related terms. I treat the different noun and verbal forms of the word as well as the phrase *'ishah zonah*, which marks the woman Rahab in the book of Joshua. I also attend to the concern of cultic prostitutes, despite the fact that recent scholarship is not univocal on the historicity of cultic or temple prostitutes in ancient Israel.

## Rahab and Modern Readers

Modern readers are predisposed to receive Rahab as a negative character because the Hebrew word *zonah* frames her in particularly negative ways. That the character is associated with sex work is evidenced by the results of a targeted, open-ended survey administered to Protestant church women. When asked, "What three words come to mind when you see or hear the word *Rahab*?" adult women assembled for a Protestant church meeting overwhelmingly identified Rahab as a prostitute or harlot.[2] Data was collated to identify those words in the first, second, and third position. Although the churchwomen responded with a range of words including *wise, hero/heroine/shero, witness, courageous/brave, negotiator,* and *protector,* a third of the women surveyed identified Rahab as *prostitute* and almost half of those surveyed identified Rahab as some combination of *prostitute, harlot,* and *streetwalker.* For these women, this association with sex work carries negative connotations. However, while *prostitute* was the first word recalled by a fourth of the survey respondents, some combination of *protector, courageous,* and *brave* was recalled in the second position by twenty-six percent of the respondents. This finding suggests modern readers may hold negative connotations in tension with positive, complimentary qualities. It seems the churchwomen initially rejected Rahab as one from whom no redeemable lessons may be learned but found positive characteristics in her when invited to give her a second look.

Conversely, another group of modern readers gravitated to the positive, redeeming characteristics of Rahab. A Bible study organized specifically for the Sex Worker Outreach Project—USA (SWOP) members explored biblical prostitution and contemporary liberation readings of the Bible to determine what the limits of those readings might be for those in the actual sex worker class.[3] Regarding the story of Rahab, these women challenged and questioned the text in ways that made room for more compassionate understandings of Rahab and other biblical characters marked by the term *zonah*.

Not surprisingly, in their reading of Joshua 2 and 6, the SWOP participants centered Rahab's prostitute identity based upon their experiences with and as sex workers. The SWOP readers accepted Rahab as a *zonah*, but they did not offer interpretations that finessed *zonah* as anything other than a sex worker. Central to many of the SWOP interpretations of Rahab's position as a sex worker is the idea that prostitution is a sacrifice for one's own survival and the survival of one's family. While the SWOP members acknowledged the negative stigma the community attached to sex work, one of the participants, Robyn, summed up the work of prostitution with an element of objectivity: "Prostitution is a job that a lot of women get into because they are starving, because they have to feed their families and take care of it."[4] Robyn's observation frames Rahab's choice to engage in sex work as a *zonah* as almost noble in its motivation.

Additionally, in their framing of the work of prostitution, the SWOP readers understood Rahab's decision to side with the enemy of the Canaanites as not necessarily linked to an allegiance to the Israelite cause. Unlike many interpreters of the text, the SWOP group minimized any theological motives for Rahab aiding the Israelite spies. For many of the SWOP readers, the stigma attached to *zonah* informed Rahab's decision to side with the Israelites. Another SWOP member, Sweet, offered a way to understand the motivation of Rahab based upon the tenuousness of her citizenship status in Jericho: "Well, because she was a prostitute, her people probably persecuted her so they really weren't her people in the first place … how can they be her people if they look down upon her, as she was 'less-than' because of the means by which she had to take care of her family. Those people were not her people."[5] For the SWOP readers, because the people of Jericho have not treated her as a full citizen, Rahab is less inclined to protect the people of Jericho.

As the churchwomen and the SWOP Bible study participants demonstrate, words matter. But perhaps the interpreter of the words matters more. The churchwomen, who are invested in a particular respectability politic regarding women's sexuality, tended to read Rahab as a "street walker" who was "fast," while members of the SWOP group, who foregrounded a woman's autonomy and ownership of her sexuality, more often identified Rahab's dignity and understood her to be motivated to provide financially for her family. This example of how different groups of people understand *zonah* in Rahab's story also hints at the notion that standard English translations of *zonah* are too flat and do not reflect the impact the use of *zonah* and related terms has on the social acceptability of its referent for modern readers. In what follows I revisit the technical vocabulary associated with *zonah* with an eye toward how the biblical writers deployed different Hebrew terms and phrases to mark women and groups of people as prostitutes, harlots, and whores.

# Name Calling: Vocabulary in Rahab's Story

Translated variously as "prostitute," "harlot," or "whore," some form of *zonah* appears in each of the three portions of the Hebrew Bible.[6] In the first *zonah* reference in the Torah, Moses identifies the money of a *zonah* as abhorrent to YHWH. Because of this abhorrence, Israelites should not use the money earned by a *zonah* to pay any vow (Deut 23:18).[7] In the book of Leviticus, Joseph argues that an Israelite father does not have the authority to force his daughter into prostitution (Lev 19:29), because she enjoys legal status as a member of her household.[8]

## Zonah *in the Former Prophets*[9]

In the Former Prophets the term *zonah* points to a woman who exists on the margins of acceptable society because she participates in sex work. Furthermore, the juxtaposition of the *zonah* to the protagonist(s) heightens the narrative tension by calling the character of the protagonist into question.[10] To begin, all of the *zonah* citations in the book of Joshua refer to Rahab. Initially, the two Israelite men enter the house of the *zonah* (Josh 2:1). Later, Joshua explains to the people that only Rahab the *zonah* and those with her will live when Jericho is destroyed (Josh 6:17). When the Israelites besiege Jericho, Joshua instructs the two men who had spied out the land to go into the *zonah*'s house and retrieve her as promised (Josh 6:22). Finally, the writer provides the commentary that Rahab the *zonah*, her family, and all who belonged to her were spared by Joshua (Josh 6:25). The writer of Joshua is careful to mark Rahab as a *zonah* throughout the conquest narrative.

In other portions of the Former Prophets such as the books of Judges and 1 Kings, the juxtaposition of the *zonah* to the narrative's protagonist again heightens the literary tension by placing the protagonist's character in question. Readers are left to question if a particular character can be the hero because he is connected to a *zonah*. In two examples, prostitutes highlight the questionable character of the male protagonist: the mention of a *zonah* highlights the questionable parentage of a warrior, and the mention of a *zonah* highlights the impulsive choices made by a warrior-hero.

In the book of Judges, the warrior Jephthah is the child of a *zonah* (Judg 11:1). By identifying his mother's profession as that of a sex worker and by suggesting his father was an indistinguishable Gileadite, the writer introduces tension in the story from the very beginning. Phyllis Trible argues Jephthah's lineage was so uncertain that only the personified district of Gilead could qualify as his sire.[11] His problematic parentage does not position Jephthah as a candidate for leadership. Born of a *zonah*, Jephthah is the unlikely hero, indeed.

The other *zonah* of note highlights the questionable character of Samson. In Samson's case, his propensity to enter new cities and immediately have sex with indiscriminate and anonymous women or women of questionable parentage signals his immature and impulsive character. Heroes are not supposed to be immature and impulsive. When Samson travels to Gaza in Judges 16, he sees "a prostitute and [goes] in to her" (Judg 16:1). This interaction with a *zonah* is particularly jarring because readers are made aware of Samson's Nazirite status in Judges 13.[12] As J. Cheryl Exum notes, Samson's effectiveness depends upon his faithfulness to his Nazirite commission, which he received in utero.[13] Moreover, a Nazirite was required to take a vow of abstinence. That Samson engages in sexual relations at all is problematic, but that he does so with a *zonah* draws attention to his questionable character.

The Former Prophets also contain the stories of two prostitutes (*zonot*) who seek adjudication by King Solomon regarding the parentage of a baby (1 Kgs 3:16), and of unnumbered prostitutes (*zonot*) who bathe in the spilled blood of King Ahab (1 Kgs 22:38). Interestingly, both of these narratives juxtapose a *zonah* against a male protagonist. Moreover, whereas the negative connotations *zonah* carries in the Former Prophets are associated with real, physical individuals, a similarly negative weight is placed upon the *zonah* who figuratively represents groups of people in the Latter Prophets.

### Zonah *in the Latter Prophets*

In the Latter Prophets the term *zonah* is deployed to personify city-states that are unfaithful to the LORD. The term's usage is set within the context of a matrix of metaphorical depictions of Israel's relationship to its God. The biblical prophets use five types of human relationships of power and punishment to describe the relationship between God and Israel: (1) judge and litigant; (2) parent and child; (3) master and slave; (4) king and vassal; and (5) husband and wife.[14] These metaphors frame the bond between God and Israel in terms of a hierarchical and authoritative relationship in which God is figured as the authority figure (judge, parent, master, king, or husband) and Israel assumes the role of the subordinate (litigant, child, slave, vassal, or wife). Additionally, these metaphorical relationships are marked by mutual obligations and responsibilities between the authority figure and the subordinate. In this system, for example, a parent is obligated to provide for, protect, and train a child and a child has the responsibility of obeying and honoring their parents (cf. Exod 20:12). Failure of the subordinate to fulfill her or his responsibility virtually guaranteed punishment, retribution, or discipline.[15] For the biblical prophets, then, God's wrath is justified when Israel does not obey God.

In Isaiah 1, the writer points to the city in chaos with its positive qualities turned upside down. John Watts suggests these qualities "are not just missing; the reverse negative qualities are present."[16] As a result of this chaos, the people have become a *zonah* (Isa 1:21). Additionally, the oracle against Tyre in Isaiah 23, the last in a series of oracles against specific nations, expresses a lament that drastically pictures the consequences of the fall of Tyre and Sidon.[17] Here, the prophet proclaims that after seventy years Tyre will live like a forgotten *zonah* (Isa 23:15-16).[18] The issue is unfaithfulness.

The marriage metaphor is popular among the Latter Prophets, who frame God as husband and the people of Israel as wife. The term *zonah* is often used in the context of the marriage metaphor to represent Israel as an out-of-order, depraved wife who engages in sexual activity beyond the bounds of marriage. In the marriage relationship, the husband promises to provide material and physical security and the wife presumably pledges her sexual loyalty and emotional faithfulness.[19] A breach occurs when one party does not fulfill his or her obligation or responsibility.

Importantly, the sexual fidelity of wives poses serious threats to patriarchal society if it is not in service to procreating legitimate heirs for their husbands.[20] By "whoring" or "prostituting" herself, the wife Israel challenges the social order and violates the founding premise of patriarchy: that a woman's sexuality does not belong to her but is the property of the men in her family.[21] Furthermore, in this schema, because a man's prestige rests in great part on his ability to control the behavior of the subordinates in his household (for instance, wives, slaves, children), the male must maintain control in order to avoid shame in the community.[22]

In Jeremiah, *zonah* refers to the people of Judah who have been unfaithful to the LORD. In the oracle of Jeremiah 3:3, the people of Judah are accused of having the forehead of a *zonah*. In the dialogue between the LORD and the prophet in Jeremiah 5:7, the LORD accuses the people of going toward the houses of the *zonah*. The implication is, Israel is married to the LORD, so any collusion with idols is like interacting with a *zonah*; idolatry is as condemnable as marital infidelity.[23] In speaking to an audience of Israelite men for whom sexual infidelity and indecency among women is considered intolerable, Jeremiah employs *zonah* imagery within the marriage metaphor, understanding his audience believes that extreme behavior in wives/Israel warrants equally extreme behavior on the part of husbands/God.[24] Ultimately, Jeremiah's message to Israel is one of redemption after judgment. Israel/the wife must be punished because her behavior is immodest at best, but after a period of punishment, God/the husband stands prepared to forgive Israel and to begin their relationship anew.[25]

In Ezekiel, *zonah* is used to mark the people of Jerusalem as the female victim of social violence brought on by their infidelity (Ezek 16:30-41).[26] Social violence in the ancient world could range from public shaming, to a lowering in status and access to power, to physical altercation. The LORD accuses Jerusalem of marital infidelity in Ezekiel 16. Here, Jerusalem is considered less honorable than a *zonah*, because Jerusalem does not reap the benefits that a prostitute would. In the prophetic metaphor, Jerusalem declined payment for its whore-like acts, gave gifts to its lovers instead of receiving gifts from its lovers, and paid for playing the whore instead of being paid for its services. In Ezekiel 23, the prophet modifies the marriage metaphor to account for the husband/God and the two sister-wives/Samaria and Jerusalem. Both Samaria and

Jerusalem receive judgment for their willful, immodest behavior, but the presentation of the extreme sexual acts of Jerusalem as the *zonah* are almost pornographic (Ezek 23:44).[27] Many interpreters argue for the porno-prophetic nature of Ezekiel 16 and 23, though challenged by those who frame Ezekiel 16 and 23 as misogynistic texts, which erroneously perpetuate negative images of women and their sexuality as pornographic propaganda.[28]

With the Ezekiel 23 narrative involving the sister-wives Oholah and Oholibah (who represent the people of Samaria and Jerusalem) it is clear that "the intention is probably to strengthen the audience's resolve that both metaphorical women, so perverse since their very maidenhood, indeed deserve the utterly degrading and devastating treatment to which they are to be exposed."[29] The first verses of Ezekiel 23 detail how Oholah and Oholibah were the victims of sexual abuse during their youth in Egypt. The *zonah* activities of the two detailed in verse 3 should be understood as acts done to them, not as acts done by them. Oholah and Oholibah were the objects of the abusive actions, not the perverse subjects. The verse may be translated, "There they [masc.] pressed the teats of their [fem.] maidenhood"; the sexual molestation inflicted upon the women then serves as a metaphor for the people's slavery in Egypt.[30] Read this way, the use of *zonah* in the pornographic metaphor deployed by Ezekiel is all the more shocking because it communicates a particularly unhealthy message that women's sexual assault is warranted—even when the rationale for such assault is illogical.

The depiction of erotic images and behaviors intended to elicit a particular sexual and emotional response mark the explicit depictions of Ezekiel as pornographic in ways other prophetic treatments are not marked. The pornographic allusions in Ezekiel include references to women's pubic hair and breasts (16:7), discussions of coital emissions (23:8), a description of a gang rape (16:37), and references to the size of the lover's sexual organ (23:20). It is clear how, "taken together, the two narratives [of Ezek 16 and 23] function as a taunt against the woman, a type of speech intended to mock, deride, and jeer at her for her lewd behavior."[31] Here, the prophets used marriage and sexuality to emphasize not only the wife's infidelity, but also the husband's absolute authority over her body and her future. Importantly, unlike in Jeremiah, with Ezekiel there is no time spent on the redemption or restoration of the unfaithful wife.

Finally, plural forms of *zonah* are present in Ezekiel wherein gifts are given to whores (*zonot*) and the people are accused of engaging in acts of whoring (*taznutay*, whorings), as in Ezekiel 16:33.

Among the Minor Prophets, the book of Hosea marks the depravity of the people by referring to prostitution and wine drinking, deploying rhetorical terms commonly used to indicate debauchery (Hos 4:11).[32] The writer of Hosea uses a form of the verb *znh*, translated variously as "playing the whore," "turning to prostitution," or "committing harlotry," to describe the negative character of the people who have been unfaithful to the LORD.[33] The daughters of the land play the whore (*tiznenah*), and men go aside to whores (*zonot*) in Hosea 4:13-14.

The book of Joel contains an account of the invasion of Israel (here, Judah and Jerusalem) followed by a restorative message focused on the renewal of the land and the animals such that "the tree bears its fruit, the fig tree and vine give their full yield" (Joel 2:22). This message speaks to the return of the fortunes of Judah and Jerusalem and offers commentary on God's compassion for God's people while also detailing the punishment of Israel's enemies for their deplorable crimes. Joel 3:3 relates how the enemies "cast lots for [God's] people, and traded boys for prostitutes [*zonah*], and sold girls for wine."[34] This use of *zonah* is particularly disturbing in its association with wicked persons who commit such atrocities. According to the Sinai covenant (see Exod 21:16), kidnapping someone for sale as a slave is punishable by death. By accusing those nations that destroyed Jerusalem of trading boys for prostitutes, the writer of Joel suggests Israel's enemies were particularly transgressive, because they acted purely for materialistic advantage—for money they spent in casual, wasteful self-indulgence. In Joel, then, *zonah* is deployed to mark a group of people as transgressive, callous, and immoral.

The writer of the book of Amos uses *zonah* to reference one "playing the whore." In Amos 7:17, Amaziah's wife will act like a prostitute of the city. Samaria's idolatry is the cause of her destruction in the book of Micah. In Micah 1:7 the LORD brings judgment against Samaria, which will include the destruction of any profits attained by acting as a *zonah*. Finally, the LORD is against Nineveh because it has acted like a *zonah* in Nahum 3:4.

In summary, biblical prophets leverage *zonah* language in metaphors intended to shape behaviors, attitudes, and reactions in the hearer. Beyond being a simply sexual term, *zonah* is used to mark transgressive behavior for an entire community. Whore and prostitute imagery in the marriage metaphor proves particularly salient and rhetorically effective for the prophets because of ancient Israel's exacting understandings of prostitutes and prostitution. From the perspective of leaders in a patriarchal society, prostitution is a threat to the all-important institution of marriage, which idealizes the husband who maintains order by exercising control over the wife. Within the marriage construct, "prostitution" signals the threat that the wife (poetically representative of the subordinate Israel in relation to the authoritative husband, God) is not performing in agreement with the marriage relationship. This threat challenges the stability of the divine-human relationship, just as actual prostitution challenges the status quo of the society.

## Zonah *in the Writings*

Similar to its use in the Former and Latter Prophets, *zonah* marks dangerous and socially unacceptable individuals in the few citations found in the Writings. The noun *zonah* is used in Proverbs when the father or teacher figure advises the son or student to avoid the *zonah* (Prov 6:26; 7:10; 23:27). The father refers to the cheap fee of a *zonah*, speaks of how dangerously enticing a *zonah* can be, and cautions the son (an upstanding young man) to avoid a *zonah* because she is a deep pit. Readers later learn that the child who squanders keeps company with prostitutes (*zonot*) in Proverbs 29:3.

### The Phrase *'Ishah Zonah*

In addition to presenting as a noun for an individual or as a verb, *zonah* is often used throughout the Bible in the phrase אשה-זונה (*'ishah zonah*, "woman prostitute," "prostitute").[35] Many of the *zonah* references cited above (including the Rahab reference in Josh 2) actually contain this phrase, *'ishah zonah*.[36] Instead of revisiting each of the occurrences of *'ishah zonah*, here I consider the popular use of the phrase in the book of Hosea. In Hosea 1:2 the LORD instructs the prophet to take for himself an אשת-זנונים (*'eshet zenunim*, wife/woman of whoredom). English translators tend to render this phrase as "a wife of whoredom." That the phrase is simply translated "prostitute" elsewhere (as in Lev 21:7; Josh 2:1; Judg 16:1; Jer 3:3; Ezek 16:30 NIV; Prov 6:26) brings attention to the English translators' decision to render such a curious image in the Hosea passage.

To be clear, this "wife of whoredom" translation seems intentional in the Hosea passage. One way to understand the "wife of whoredom" language here is to consider that "prostituting woman" is idiomatic syntactically and sufficiently pejorative without firmly conveying the idea, contrary to fact, that Yahweh commanded Hosea to marry a professional prostitute.[37] While I agree the translation is pejorative, I disagree with this interpretive approach's suggestion that the translation does not directly convey the idea that God commanded Hosea to marry a prostitute. The Hebrew writer seems to place even more emphasis on the *zonah* character of the wife by deploying the construct "wife of."

Readers are left to ask the question, "Wife of what?" Considering how, as I have argued previously, prostitution, harlotry, and whoredom run in diametrical opposition to the woman's role in marriage for the ancient Israelite, "prostitute" should be read as less harsh than "wife of whoredom." Rhetorically, the oxymoronic or incongruent nature of the phrase "wife of whoredom" punctuates the extreme to which God wants Hosea to go in an effort to illustrate God's extreme love for Israel.

## Zonah and Cultic Prostitution

Finally, *zonah* is part of the construction of the concept of a cultic prostitute. Although beyond the scope of this chapter, there are multiple perspectives on the historical existence of sacred prostitutes.[38] One can accept that women functioned as prostitutes, but maintain that cultic prostitution did not exist in ancient Israel.[39] A major scholarly position in favor of the existence of sacred prostitutes asserts these prostitutes were called *zonoth* because they were connected with the worship of foreign deities. This perspective takes *zonoth* to imply the idea of illicit intercourse. From the point of view of the prophetic reformers, any commerce with foreign gods was illegitimate, and hence certainly with the sacred harlots devoted to those gods.[40] An extension of this angle considers the primary meaning of *zonah* as prostitution, whether it is extended to any other type of female sexual behavior considered deviant or whether the primary meaning encompasses a whole range of acts that differ from the norm, which then narrows down into prostitution in the prophetic material because any unusual behavior is considered as bad as prostitution.[41]

Considering the evidence from ancient Near Eastern and Greco-Roman texts and early Christian authors, a dissenting perspective avers that the majority of sources that have been interpreted as pertaining to sacred prostitution actually have nothing to do with this institution. Within the ancient Near Eastern material, for example, members of the upper classes would dedicate an eldest daughter to *naditu*-hood to pray for the family. The *naditu* (which linguistically means "woman who lies fallow") were devoted to a dominant male deity of the city; however, the data emphatically suggests nothing sexual was involved in this devotion. Instead, the data points to the *naditu* as celibate members of the community. It is thus highly unlikely that the *naditu* were prostitutes of any kind.[42]

I side with those who argue that the idea of cultic prostitutes took on a life of its own as a metaphor among the biblical prophets.[43] While there may be evidence of cultic prostitutes in the ancient Near East, the historical reality of temple or cultic prostitutes is less important than the idea of the mixing of the sacred and the profane among foreign cultures. For the Israelites, the distinction between sacred and profane was an important boundary. Most particularly, the power of the metaphor (which turns on the scandal of deviant social behavior) relies on the disdain the Israelites had for the social practices of non-Israelites. The association with a non-Israelite practice—real or imagined—would have made for a persuasive argument to the Israelite community.

## Conclusion

This brief treatment of the term *zonah* demonstrates that words matter. While I am most interested in Rahab as a *zonah* in the Joshua narrative, this word in its many forms is found throughout the biblical text. When used in a concrete or literal manner, a *zonah* is an individual who is held in contempt by the Israelite community because her presence threatens the patriarchal status quo by pointing to women who control their own bodies in ways that "acceptable" Israelite women do not. There are no references to a male *zonah* in the Hebrew Bible.[44] The term *zonah* therefore is weighted with negative connotations that only apply to women.

The association of the *zonah* with sex work contributes to this disparaging treatment of the individual within the biblical world. Members of the Israelite community view the *zonah* with condescension; the *zonah* therefore exists on the margins of the community. In the case of Rahab, her social standing and physical location each position her on the margins of the community. As a *zonah* who lives in or on the wall of the city, Rahab exists as far away from the center of Jericho as one can and still be considered a citizen of the city.

When used metaphorically, *zonah* marks unfaithful people (regarding marital infidelity and spiritual apostasy), and supports the negative connotation of prostitute and the community members' jettisoning of the individual. The biblical prophets use *zonah* metaphorically when they imagine Israel as the subordinate wife of God, the authoritative husband. Isaiah speaks of the faithful city that has become a *zonah* (Isa 1:21), and Ezekiel speaks of Israel's enemies going into the Israelite community as one goes into a *zonah* (Ezek 23:44).

The term *zonah*, with all of its negative connotations, undergirds many discussions about Rahab. This is because most retellings of her story draw attention to her designation as a prostitute. Even without benefit of the nuances of the Hebrew language, these negative images for prostitute, harlot, and whore impact modern readers' understanding of the character Rahab. The examples of the churchwomen and the SWOP women speak to how modern readers think differently about Rahab the prostitute. While the latter demonstrate empathy toward Rahab's situation, most modern readers do not share their experiences and so, when Rahab is introduced to the majority of modern readers as a *zonah*, they are predisposed to view her negatively.

## CHART 1
### English Translations of *Zonah*

The following chart demonstrates how English translators render *zonah* as some combination of "prostitute," "whore," and "harlot."

|     | Gen 34:31 | Hos 4:13-14 | Prov 6:26 |
| --- | --- | --- | --- |
| NIV | But they replied, "Should he have treated our sister like a **prostitute?**" | Therefore your daughters **turn to prostitution** ... your daughters when they **turn to prostitution** ... because the men themselves consort with **harlots** ... | For a **prostitute** can be had for a loaf of bread ... |

|  | Gen 34:31 | Hos 4:13-14 | Prov 6:26 |
|---|---|---|---|
| **NKJV** | But they said, "Should he treat our sister like a **harlot**?" | Therefore your daughters **commit harlotry**... your daughters when they **commit harlotry**... For the men themselves go apart with **harlots**... | For by means of a **harlot** A man is reduced to a crust of bread... |
| **NRSV** | But they said, "Should our sister be treated like a **whore**?" | Therefore your daughters **play the whore**... your daughters when they **play the whore**... for the men themselves go aside with **whores**... | for a **prostitute**'s fee is only a loaf of bread... |

## CHART 2
### Rahab Survey Question and Results

This chart demonstrates the responses of survey participants when asked,

"What three words come to mind when you see or hear the word Rahab?"

| WORDS | | |
|---|---|---|
| **1st word** | **2nd word** | **3rd word** |
| Prostitute | Helper | Believed |
| Prostitute | Protector | Brave |
| Wise | Courageous | Shero |
| Other | Walking | Other |
| Prostitute | Red cord | Human |
| Heroine | Harlot | Servant |

| WORDS | | |
|---|---|---|
| **1st word** | **2nd word** | **3rd word** |
| Harlot | "Fast" | Obedient |
| Prostitute | | |
| Street walker | Brave | Courageous |
| Bible | Queen Esther | Boaz |
| Bible | Queen Esther | Boaz |
| Courageous | Bold | Belief |
| God | Blessings | Praise |
| Witness | Protector | Unselfish |
| Cord | Helper | Promise-Keeper |
| Prostitute | Protector | Provider |
| Catholic | | |
| Courageous | Negotiator | Protector |
| Redeemed | Trusted God | Daring |
| Saved her family | Woman moved by God | Gave cover to God's people |
| Jewish Ancestor | | |
| Prostitute | Protector | Wife |
| Protector | Prostitute | Preparer |
| Hero | Rope | Prostitute |

—2—

# RESEARCHING RAHAB
## Major Streams of Investigation

## Introduction

This chapter lays the groundwork for a discussion of the many ways people have read and interpreted Rahab's story. My goal is not to argue for a particular interpretation or even to offer a new way of reading. No. In this chapter I simply bring the reader up to speed on the many different ways others have approached Rahab and her story. The different angles or reading strategies represent the many voices—the polyphonic aspect—of interpretive possibilities. To that end, I begin by spotlighting the major approaches to Rahab and encourage the reader to see other reasoned perspectives on Rahab that may be overshadowed by the more popular positions but that add a richness to the study of Rahab in their own right.

## Respectability in the Biblical World

Modern conversations about Rahab and her story happen amidst a series of other conversations, and these larger conversations inform the entry point for a discussion about Rahab. The first of three major approaches to Rahab exists within the more general conversation about acceptability or respectability in the biblical world; this conversation is undergirded by the presumption that males rightly control female bodies and embodiment. When interpreting Rahab's story, then, these interpretations focus on the woman of Jericho based upon her designation as one engaged in the sex-work industry. Rahab's characterization as a harlot or prostitute entails conversations around prostitution as improper sexual behavior, the difference between sacred and secular prostitution, and foreign women's bodies as a proxy for land.

Generally speaking, women and their behavior are limited to classifications as either socially acceptable (a virgin or a wife) or socially objectionable (a prostitute).[1] The virgin Rebekah (Gen 24) and wives like Rachel and Hannah (Gen 29 and 1 Sam 1) are viewed as pillars of acceptable society, while prostitutes like Tamar (Gen 38), Jephthah's mother (Judg 11), and Hosea's wife Gomer (Hos 1) are considered outcasts in the world of the biblical text. The biblical writer marks Rahab with the Hebrew term *zonah*, which is translated "harlot" or "prostitute."[2] This *zonah* designation, therefore, relegates Rahab to the margins of decency.

Prostitution, defined as the act of offering sexual favors for pay, is considered illicit because it is a sexual act performed by women outside of marriage.[3] Moreover, certain interpretations of Rahab's story attend to the semantic range of *zonah* within the Hebrew Bible in general and the Joshua narrative in particular. These interpretations conclude that the semantic range of the Hebrew term covers a wide variety of sexual behaviors that are considered improper. These sexual deeds are read against the law of Deuteronomy 22, which details the boundaries of acceptable female behavior. The variety of improper sexual behaviors includes those of the Levite's concubine who supposedly engaged in deviant behavior when she left her husband (Judg 19) and any woman who commits adultery. Examples of the association of *zonah* with the crossing of acceptable boundaries include Genesis 34, in which Dinah's brothers seem upset that Shechem has treated their sister like a *zonah*, and Proverbs 23, in which a *zonah* is considered a "deep pit." The negative connotations of female sexuality outside social standards is further reinforced by the numerous poetic metaphors for religious apostasy that draw on the language of sexual infidelity in prophetic texts such as Jeremiah, Ezekiel, and Hosea.

Readings of Rahab's story that highlight her faith or point to the inclusivity of YHWH and the Israelites all turn on the axis of Rahab being a prostitute.[4] These readings of Rahab clearly position her as a sex worker of some sort with the understanding that sex work is an outcast or marginalized field of employment. But if Rahab is a prostitute, what type of prostitute is she?

Rahab's stated occupation is complicated by the idea that there may have been different types of prostitutes in the ancient world. As noted, most understand a prostitute to be a sex worker doing business in the public square. Still others who treat Rahab's story frame her as a cultic or religious prostitute. A cultic or sacred or temple prostitute is simply a prostitute whose activities are carried out in religious contexts. In the ancient Near East those who performed sex acts in exchange for money that was committed to deities such as Aštarte and Ištar may have been considered sacred prostitutes. Readings that mark Rahab as a cultic prostitute, despite the fact that the Hebrew term generally used for cultic prostitutes, *qedeshah*, does not appear in Rahab's narrative, suggest she was more than a generic, "run of the mill" harlot.[5]

Not everyone agrees that cultic prostitution existed in the

ancient world. One way of reading the data associated with cultic prostitution in antiquity suggests that the idea of cultic prostitution is nothing more than a literary construct.[6] Those who discount the validity of sacred prostitution in antiquity identify an artificial conglomeration of ideas that have been assembled into the *image* of a ritual or institution or practice of cultic prostitution. It seems the various literary data that have given rise to the idea of sacred prostitution may actually have meant something else in their ancient contexts.

Among those who study sacred or cultic prostitution in ancient Near Eastern and Mediterranean societies, some approach the evidence by examining the language or vocabulary used to mark these individuals in Sumerian, Akkadian, Ugaritic, and Hebrew texts. Here, cultic or religious prostitution can only be implied because many of the words identified as "sacred prostitute" in the ancient Near Eastern languages are actually of uncertain definition.[7] Archaeological investigations render similar results. For example, in late antiquity few texts used to construct the myth of sacred prostitution actually have anything to do with it.

It seems individuals already familiar with the myth read it into passages that somehow involved religious ritual and sexuality that might have been termed "sacred sex." The problem here is that not even the "sacred sex" really existed.[8] The myth of cultic prostitution spread like a computer virus.[9] The idea of cultic prostitution became so popular among those who studied ancient Near Eastern societies and gained so much momentum that the adoption of the idea was nearly impossible to stop.

Finally, while a significant conversation revolves around Rahab's connection to sex work, other approaches to the text concentrate on women and their bodies as proxies for land; specifically, land that was targeted for invasion. It goes without saying that Rahab serves as the catalyst of the conquest, but one way of reading the text foregrounds her as a prostitute and suggests that the two Israelite spies' mission to view the land was really a directive to look upon the women of the land.[10] This interpretive strategy nods toward the transactional nature of prostitution. In this way, if the taking of the land is a way of taking the woman, the description, or explanation, of Rahab as a *zonah* further undergirds the message that sex is available for purchase in the new land of Jericho.[11]

In all these treatments of Rahab and her story, while the dominant voice focuses the reader's attention on Rahab's position on the fringe of society due to her association with sex work, the less dominant voices—those relegated to the background—encourage readings that consider other plausible interpretive options. The background voices add sonic textures to this conversation with harmonies that press for proof of the allegation that Rahab was a prostitute and ask questions around the morality of prostitution in the ancient world. At any rate, the prostitute moniker impacts readers' understanding of Rahab as a character on the margins of acceptable society.

## Ethnic Identity or Group Affiliation

The second of the popular streams of inquiry about Rahab highlights her ethnic identity or group affiliation. From the perspective of the Israelite writer, as a citizen of Jericho, Rahab is a foreign woman. The Israelite community had particular constrictions or rules about interaction with foreigners, especially foreign women. For example, legal prescriptions deny foreigners access to political power and cultic privileges (Deut 17:15 and Exod 12:43). The Israelites are suspicious of foreigners because they may prove to be daunting enemies during wartime or, worse yet, cause the followers of YHWH to go after other gods (Neh 9:2).

Foreign women are particularly dangerous, because they are assumed to lure the men of Israel into idolatry. This assumption explains the prohibition in Deuteronomy 7:3 against marrying foreign women. Many reading strategies deployed against the Joshua 2 text that mark Rahab as a foreigner ground their perspective in either the physical location of Rahab's home on the boundary of Jericho or her designation as a member of the community of Jericho. In actuality, these readings associate Rahab with foreignness by subtly conflating her proximity to strangers, her treasonous act against the Canaanite empire, and her alleged sexual activity.

Certain interpretations of Rahab's story understand her home, which is located in the wall that bounds the city of Jericho, as a waystation for foreign travelers—a tavern or an inn. These readings recognize similarities to ancient Near Eastern literature, highlighting the connection between innkeepers and foreigners and then drawing an interpretive line between innkeepers and Rahab.[12] In this way Rahab encounters the Israelite foreigners in Joshua 2 in the same way the tavern keeper Siduri encounters travelers in *The Epic of Gilgamesh*.[13] Importantly, not only did the profession uniquely put innkeepers in direct contact with foreign visitors, but these hospitality industry professionals had an important responsibility to the monarchy. Specifically, the innkeeper was required to notify the palace of any stranger who might come to the inn, especially a foreigner engaged in hostile activity. When read from this perspective, Rahab's misleading of the king's envoy becomes a treasonous crime against the nation, which may have even been punishable by death.[14]

An entire stream of inquiry around the foreigner status of Rahab understands her as a Native Woman.[15] This way of reading generally recognizes a literary trope of the hypersexualized foreign or native woman operating in the text. In these Native Woman stories the women (1) fall in love with, have sex with, or marry the conqueror; (2) save the conqueror(s) by going against their own people; (3) embrace the conqueror's culture as the first step of conversion; and (4) are co-opted by the conqueror's culture.[16] Modern readers may recognize this trope in Disney's "Pocahontas" character.

These presentations of Rahab as a foreign Native Woman include the celebration of her as deserving a place in Israelite society. Reading with the text, it is precisely *in spite of* her shameful designation as a prostitute that Rahab morphs into a figure of respectability in both Jewish and Christian traditions. Specifically, Rahab appears in Jewish legend as Joshua's wife and the ancestress of prophets and priests like Huldah and Jeremiah. Similarly, Christian interpretations such as Hebrews 11:31 and James 2:25 emphasize Rahab's sexual deviance, prophetic activity, and, naturally, her conversion.[17]

Interpretive approaches that marginalize Rahab as a Canaanite prostitute foreground how her very being challenges Israelite notions of good and right. Here, the alleged practice of "whoring after idols," which is attributed to foreign communities like the Canaanite citizenry, threatens Israelite moral and religious sensibilities. In these sorts of readings, by establishing Rahab as "an extreme" Canaanite (a woman diametrically opposed to the image of a respectable Israelite woman), the narrator sets up the reader to expect nothing positive from Rahab because she is a Canaanite.[18] Indeed, when the one whom readers expect little of literally saves the day for Israel, it is intentionally surprising.

When one shifts one's interpretive attention away from such

orientations toward understandings of Rahab that place her in the spotlight and objectify her as a foreign woman, it is clear the only way one can credibly mark Rahab as a "foreign" woman is to read from the colonizing perspective of the Israelite writer. This is understandable, because modern readers have been conditioned to read with the grain of the story as received and to side with the victor. Nevertheless, to view Rahab as a foreigner is akin to standing on foreign soil and marking the indigenous people as strangers in their own land. A fresh read of the text only renders Rahab a foreigner when she enters the Israelite camp after the destruction of Jericho (Josh 6).

## Heroine

Finally, the third angle through which many read Rahab and her story celebrates her as a heroine. Leveraging the "harlot with a heart of gold" trope, these explorations of Joshua 2 and 6 frame Rahab as an unexpected hero. One popular approach to Rahab in this way deploys the calamity motif, which sets the reader up to expect that disaster will fall upon the spies, and that Joshua's mission will be thwarted—were it not for a hero(ine).[19]

The elements of a calamity motif permeate Rahab's story. In Joshua 2 spying turns to pursuit when those sent to view the land become the object of the king's messengers, who pursue them as far as the fords (Josh 2:7). Adding to the calamity motif, innuendo regarding inappropriate sexuality marks the Israelites' entrance into Jericho: the spies are dispatched from Shittim, which is where the Israelites had sexual relationships with Moabite women (Num 25:1). Furthermore, the biblical writer's use of Hebrew terms like בוא (bo`, "come in, come, go in, go"), שכב (shakhav, "lie down"), and ידע (yada`, "know") are examples of the pervasive sexual imagery in the text.[20] Readers are intended to think that the Israelite spies are going to thwart their mission by violating standards of holiness.

Finally, strange visitors, the night setting, and characters escaping a doomed city evoke the story of Lot and his visitors in Genesis 19. In line with the calamity motif, the night setting in both stories strongly denotes an atmosphere of danger.[21] Pursuit, sexual innuendo, and the presence of darkness all conspire to predispose the reader to expect some disaster or calamity will befall the spies. But Rahab's actions of hiding the spies and misdirecting the king's messengers prevent the calamity and set her up as the unlikely hero.

Other approaches to Rahab as a hero simply highlight the general heroic characteristics that she possesses. Like any good hero, Rahab is brave, determined, strategically focused, deliberate in her subterfuge, and clear-headed in her actions. Rahab demonstrates bravery when, by assisting the enemy of the city of Jericho, she commits treason. She demonstrates determination and strategic focus in her interaction with the king's messengers and in her negotiation with the Israelite spies. Rahab is deliberate in her subterfuge to save the lives of the Israelite spies, and she is clear-headed in ensuring the safety of her family members.

Alternative readings of Rahab as a hero may ask who or what created the situation or circumstances that necessitated heroic action in the first place. When read from the perspective of the Jericho community, Rahab should not be celebrated but persecuted.

## Other Interpretive Approaches

This chapter reminds the reader that there are many interpretive approaches to Rahab and her story. Moreover, while these major ways of reading the biblical narrative have long and entrenched histories, they are not the only ways of attending to Rahab and her story. Undoubtedly, there are many more ways to read Rahab. The three paths described here leave many questions unanswered, inviting us to explore those plausible alternative interpretative approaches to the Joshua narrative.

—3—

# RECASTING RAHAB
## Reading Rahab with African American Literature

## Introduction

Theologian, educator, and mystic Howard Thurman tells the story of how his grandmother, a devout Christian, rejected the words of Paul:

> When I was older and was half through college, I chanced to be spending a few days at home near the end of summer vacation. With a feeling of great temerity I asked her one day why it was that she would not let me read any of the Pauline letters. What she told me I shall never forget. "During the days of slavery," she said, "the master's minister would occasionally hold services for the slaves. Old man McGhee was so mean that he would not let a Negro minister preach to his slaves. Always the white minister used as his text something from Paul. At least three or four times a year he used as a text: 'Slaves, be obedient to them that are your masters . . . , as unto Christ.' Then he would go on to show how it was God's will that we were slaves and how, if we were good and happy slaves, God would bless us. I promised my Maker that if I ever learned to read and if freedom ever came, I would not read that part of the Bible."[1]

Thurman's grandmother did not include Paul's words among the religious documents she valued as special, valid, official, or fundamental for her understanding of The Divine. For Thurman's grandmother, Paul's words may have been biblical, but they were not part of her personal canon. Just as Thurman's grandmother established her personal canon, so have members of the African American literary community selected writers and writings as part of the canon of African American literature. For example, W. E. B. Du Bois's *The Souls of Black Folk*; Richard Wright's *Native Son*; Ralph Ellison's *Invisible Man*; Zora Neale Hurston's *Their Eyes Were Watching God*; Carter G. Woodson's *The Mis-Education of the Negro*; Maya Angelou's *I Know Why the Caged Bird Sings*; and Booker T. Washington's *Up From Slavery: An Autobiography* are all considered indispensable contributions to the expansive African American literary canon. These works are canon because, in some way, they help their readers make meaning out of life's circumstances. For many, writings from the African American literary canon are similar to the books of the biblical canon: they are special, valid, official, or fundamental for an understanding of the world marked by a keen awareness of oppressive forces as well as a faithful, hopeful resilience.

The biblical narrative that opens in Joshua 2 and concludes in Joshua 6 is not unfamiliar to most students of the Bible. It is also canonical for many readers of the biblical text. Rahab and her story are taken up in movies, art, music, and church Bible studies, because so many find value and meaning in that story. This chapter continues the previous chapter's description of the major strands of biblical scholarship, but this time through the lens of identity. Then I explore what it might look like to read Rahab's story alongside an African American literary canon. Specifically, I argue that Rahab, like characters in Nella Larsen's novels *Quicksand*

and *Passing*, is "passing" in Joshua 2. In this way, this chapter connects two canons.

## Rahab in the Biblical Canon

As mentioned in the last chapter, to date, most thinking has focused on these elements of Rahab's identity: her role as a hero, her designation as a prostitute, and her hypersexualization as a foreign woman.[2] In her 1989 article "The Harlot as Heroine: Narrative Art and Social Presupposition in Three Old Testament Texts," Phyllis Bird claims Rahab's *hesed* or radical hospitality toward the Israelites secures her safety and the safety of her family.[3] Rahab is a heroine because she helps the Israelites escape by letting them down through a window in the wall.[4] Aaron Sherwood presents Rahab as a hero when he argues that she acts in the role of *deus ex machina*: time and again, Rahab saves the day. As heroine, Rahab appears in every scene and is given the majority of the dialogue in Joshua 2.[5] Ultimately, in almost superhero-like fashion, Rahab swoops in and (through astute negotiation with the Israelite spies) makes sure her family survives the destruction of Jericho.[6]

Ironically, while Rahab is presented as a hero, she is marked by a term that is not associated with heroism. Although the Hebrew word *zonah* (generally translated "prostitute," "harlot," or "whore") regularly points to a sexual exchange, as in the stories of Dinah and Tamar in Genesis,[7] the term does not always point to sexual activity. Athalya Brenner-Idan reminds her readers that the noun *zonah* ("prostitute") is derived from the root *znh,* which can also denote "leave" or "turn aside (from God)."[8] It is this use of *zonah* for female practitioners of fertility rites and their actions that readers find in the Latter Prophets. For example, in Isaiah 1:21, the writer uses figurative language to condemn the city's infidelity—or turning away from YHWH—in the statement, "How the faithful city has become a whore! She that was full of justice, righteousness lodged in her—but now murderers!" Similarly, the LORD announces the punishment of the religious unfaithful of Judah in an oracle found in Ezekiel 23:44: "For they have gone in to her, as one goes in to a whore. Thus they went in to Oholah and to Oholibah, wanton women."

As previously discussed, in the Former Prophets, *zonah* is usually connected to some mention of sexual activity or with someone with a sexualized history. This is the case in the stories of Jephthah's mother and of Samson.[9] Jephthah's mother is a *zonah*, and she apparently is so sexually active that no one knows who Jephthah's father is.[10] Additionally, Samson has sex with a *zonah* in Judges 16. Here *zonah* is attached to a character with an established sexual pattern (that Samson had a reputation "with the ladies" is widely accepted).

Interestingly, Rahab is marked as a *zonah*, but there is no textual evidence that she engages in a sex act. Although there is no mention of sexual activity in her story as in the story of Dinah, no evidence of sex in the form of a subsequent pregnancy as in the story of Tamar, and no mention of her sexualized history as in the stories of Jephthah's mother and Samson, the biblical writers foreground Rahab as a prostitute, a harlot, or a whore. I follow the reading of those scholars who suggest that the designation of Rahab as a *zonah* is a rhetorical device of the Deuteronomistic Historian, deployed to persuade the reader to understand her as the marginalized Other.[11]

Regarding the hypersexualization of Rahab, Randall C. Bailey takes up Rahab's story as a backdrop to highlight a threefold strategy executed by the biblical writers to destabilize a group of people.

The first strategy, and the one of interest here, is the sexualization of indigenous persons to legitimate their dispossession and annihilation.[12] Bailey argues convincingly that the writer of Joshua destabilizes the Canaanites and in effect legitimates their oppression by presenting Rahab as a prostitute. Bradley Crowell picks up on Bailey's point, arguing that "the first Canaanite woman is hypersexualized as a foreign woman not by anything that she does or says, but by the narrator's emphasis on her occupation: she is a *zonah*, a prostitute."[13]

Beyond these three considerations of Rahab's identity as characterized in Joshua, recent scholarship has also looked at Rahab as she is presented in the rabbinic midrash,[14] then analyzed her story through various cultural lenses,[15] and even produced creative retellings of Rahab's story in the first person.[16] What scholarship has not done is interrogate issues of identity in relation to Rahab in ways that are distinctly meaningful to me and others like me as female members of the African American community. Although Charles Copher (considered the father of Black Biblical Studies) treated the Black presence in the Bible in his groundbreaking works, he was not concerned with the female character of Joshua 2 or with the gendered and racial dynamics at play in her story.[17] This opens an opportunity to explore these aspects of identity in the story of Rahab. Specifically, I am interested in how perceptions of the identity of Rahab as an individual—not the identity of the community (scholars such as Daniel Hawk already focus on identity formation of the Israelite community)—play out in the book of Joshua.

## Rahab and the African American Literary Canon

This chapter recasts Rahab's story using the lens of "passing." I propose that Rahab's ambiguous identity, movement in the form of constant border crossing, and an element of secrecy or threat of exposure all support the claim that—much like two characters in the novels of Nella Larsen—the character Rahab is passing in the book of Joshua.

After defining "passing," I will identify its markers based upon the work of Nella Larsen. Here, I will use the characters Helga Crane from her novel *Quicksand* and Clare Kendry from her novel *Passing* as my exemplars. I will then map passing elements onto the story in the book of Joshua to demonstrate my case. What I am proposing is a womanist interpretive study that seeks to center the experiences of Black women—in this case, the characters of Helga and Clare—as its hermeneutic, its interpreatvie principle. While I recognize that other communities engage in passing, I am using African American literature as a mechanism to illuminate the particular experiences of Black women. Finally, I conclude this examination with a look forward into potential research possibilities.

## Defining "Passing"

The historian George Fredrickson dates the phrase and phenomenon of "passing" to at least the late eighteenth century, where it was an "institutionalized . . . characteristic of the Cape Colony of South Africa."[18] Later, in 1962 sociologist Gunnar Myrdal provided a working definition of "passing." According to Myrdal, "passing" means that a Negro becomes a white man, that is, moves from the lower to the higher caste. Myrdal states that "in the American caste order, this can be accomplished only by the deception of the white people with whom the passer comes to associate and by a conspiracy of silence on the part of other Negroes who might know about it."[19] Passing then includes some element of identity ambiguity and an element of secrecy.

In the introduction to her 1996 edited volume *Passing and the Fictions of Identity*, English professor Elaine Ginsberg explains that the idea of passing has etymological roots in the Latin noun *passus*, or a "step." In its verbal form, the primary significations of *passus* were thus "to step, pace, or walk." Passing then comes "to denote progression or moving on from place to place." In the case of race passing in the United States, this idea of movement is recovered in the implicit reference to a metaphoric geography of race. One crosses or passes over the color line dividing black and white.[20] Passing involves movement.

The practice of passing is not unfamiliar to most African Americans, because many know of family members who have passed or are familiar with historical incidents of passing.[21] As an example, in an effort to escape slavery, William Craft had his wife, Ellen (who was nearly white), pose as an invalid white gentleman and pretend to be his master so the two might leave Macon, GA. Then there is the story of Charlotte Giles and Harriet Eglin, who, in the antebellum period, wore suits of mourning with heavy black veils and journeyed by train to Philadelphia. The two women were so undetectable that when one of their masters boarded the train and asked for their names, he did not recognize the women dressed in mourning clothes.[22] Ambiguity is a marker of passing; people are unable to determine the identity of the passer.

For the purposes of my examination of Rahab and her story, I define passing as the act of moving across culturally constructed boundary markers that otherwise limit one's social status. This act presents a real danger should the passer be exposed due to the community anxiety produced by identity ambiguity.

## Passing in Nella Larsen's Novels

Born to a white Danish mother and Black West Indian father, Nella Larsen was a respected novelist in the Harlem Renaissance literary movement. Larsen published *Quicksand* in 1928 and *Passing* in 1929. In *Quicksand*, Helga Crane's story contains two of the passing markers I have identified for this chapter: identity ambiguity and movement. Martha Cutter states that Helga "repeatedly attempts to find a true identity, only to learn that no such thing exists, only a variety of social roles."[23] In Chicago, the key to the ambiguous nature of this identity is provided by Mrs. Hayes-Rore, who hears Helga's tragic family history and comments, "I wouldn't mention that my people are white, if I were you. Colored people won't understand it, and after all it's your own business."[24]

In Harlem, Helga's adoption of her role as a member of Black middle-class society is so immersive that for many months she does not question this identification at all.[25] When Helga realizes she does not "fit" in Harlem, she journeys to Denmark to reconnect with her mother's side of the family. Here, the community hands Helga a role to play. Helga's aunt determines "the role that Helga was to play" is that of an exotic Other.[26] These examples gesture toward identity ambiguity as a central element in Helga Crane's story. Helga's identity is in perpetual flux throughout the novel.

Likewise, identity is unsure or unstable in Larsen's second novel, *Passing,* in which readers are introduced to Clare Kendry, who is living her life as a white woman. Clare's story is illustrative of all three elements of passing: identity ambiguity, movement, and secrecy. For the sake of brevity, I offer that Clare's identity ambiguity begins with the lore surrounding her disconnection from her community of origin. After Clare's father dies, a young Irene Redfield reflects on the whereabouts of her friend. Larsen writes: "For there had been rumours. . . . There was the one about Clare Kendry's having been seen at the dinner hour in a fashionable hotel in company with another woman and two men, all of them white. And dressed! And there was another, which told of her driving in Lincoln Park with a man, unmistakably white, and evidently rich. Packard limousine, chauffeur in livery, and all that. There had been others whose context Irene could no longer recollect, but all pointing in the same glamorous direction."[27] Clare's passing is so well executed that, later in the novel, readers learn her husband, John Bellew, is unaware that his wife and her light-skinned friends are Black!

It seems that after the death of her Black father Clare Kendry began to disguise her racial identity, and that decision required Clare to move and remain on the move. Indeed, much of the plot of *Passing* turns on the second element of passing, movement. In her attempts to traverse boundary markers, Clare Kendry is always in motion. Clare moves from her childhood neighborhood in Chicago, to live "with some relatives, aunts or cousins two or three times removed, over on the west side."[28] She moves from Chicago to NYC with her husband John Bellew, and they travel internationally. In all of this physical movement, Clare moves across socioeconomic boundaries. The move from her impoverished childhood home (in which her father was a janitor) to John Bellew's home (which affords Clare the luxuries of a life lived on multiple continents) point to this movement. Moreover, in her act of passing Clare transgresses racial boundaries. Even Clare's insistence on attending Felise's party in Harlem at the end of the story is an example of boundary crossing. Clare—who has been passing all this time—literally steps back over the race line to attend this gathering of well-to-do Blacks in Harlem.

Similarly, in *Quicksand*, Helga Crane is constantly moving. She moves back and forth across geographic boundaries when she relocates to Chicago, to New York, to Denmark, and eventually to Alabama. She moves between social classes when she leaves her job as a schoolteacher at an elite boarding school in the South and becomes unemployed in the North. As a foreigner in Denmark, Helga traffics among the social elite; she then transgresses another social boundary when she becomes the rural preacher's wife in Alabama.

Finally, passing contains an element of secrecy: the true racial identity of the passer must be kept a secret. The novel *Passing* contains the more overt examples of this third element of passing.[29] Clare's secret triggers the novel's tragic ending. As the drama of the narrative moves to climax, the revelation of Clare's secret becomes central. When Clare's white husband arrives at the Harlem party demanding to see his wife, the danger associated with the exposure of Clare's passing produces anxiety for the reader and for other characters in the room. When Bellew spots his wife he exclaims, "So you're a nigger, a damned dirty nigger!" Clare's secret is exposed. The denouement of the novel is marked by chaos and confusion. The exposure of Clare's secret proves deadly.

## Passing in Rahab's Story

Returning to the biblical text, Rahab demonstrates all three elements of passing. Rahab's identity is unclear. She is a Canaanite, but in her engagement with the spies she presents herself as loyal to the Israelites. Rahab is a citizen of Jericho, but, in an act that constitutes treason, she intentionally misleads the representatives of the commonwealth, the king's messengers. Rahab is a woman in the patriarchal ancient world, but she does not appear to be under the authoritative gaze or protective arm of the male head of household (her father). Rahab is called a *zonah*, but she does not engage in the activities associated with a prostitute. Moreover, the veiled language and sexual innuendo that permeate Rahab's narrative add to the ambiguity.

The writer of Joshua informs the reader in 2:1 that the spies go to the house of the prostitute and *shkhv* ("lie" or "lie down") there.[30] Do they simply lodge there for the night or do they have sexual relations there? The text is unclear. Is the red cord of Joshua 2:18 simply a visual indicator for the Israelites to easily recognize Rahab's house when they do their recovery work later in Joshua 6? Is the red cord meant to signify a Passover, reminiscent of the salvific blood on the door in Exodus 12:13? Or is the red cord a symbol of a woman's red lips? A great deal of ambiguity exists in Rahab's story.

Movement, margins, and transgressing boundaries are central to Rahab's story. People are constantly moving across thresholds in Joshua 2. The spies cross the territorial demarcation line when they breach the city wall and enter Jericho. The messengers cross over the physical boundary of the city gate and geographic boundaries of the land between Jericho and the Jordan River when they go out to pursue the spies "on the way to the Jordan as far as the fords" (2:7). Rahab and the spies each traverse vertical boundaries when they go up onto her rooftop, and the spies travel back across the line of demarcation when they leave Rahab's house. In all of this, Rahab and the Israelite spies ostensibly move back and forth from spaces of security to danger. Furthermore, marginalized by her physical location (her house is literally on the margins of Jericho) and her stated sex-worker profession (prostitution places her beyond the boundaries of acceptable Israelite womanhood), Rahab exists in a space of liminality.

Finally, Rahab demonstrates the third element of passing: the exposure of a secret poses a threat. Most obviously, Rahab would surely be punished should the king's messengers learn she is harboring enemy spies. Given the high-stakes nature of enemy infiltration in the conquest narrative, Rahab's punishment would surely be death. Rahab misdirects the king's military retinue so as not to risk exposing the secret of the Israelite spies. Rahab's sleight-of-hand exchange with the king's messengers also masks the secret of her community allegiance. Not only is she keeping the identity of the men a secret, but Rahab also conceals the fact that she is loyal to the Israelites.

In Joshua 2 the display of the red cord is a covert act designed to reveal the location of Rahab's house for the Israelite rescue operation. Given the attention the king's retinue is now paying to Rahab and her house, the cord cannot draw too much attention. That cord and its placement must be discreet—revealing and concealing at the same time. The secret that Rahab and her household have been designated for survival when Jericho falls to Israel must not be exposed. Keeping the secret is a matter of life and death.

## Conclusion

As an African American woman, I am fascinated by Rahab and her story. In this chapter I have read her story through the lens of the cultural phenomenon of passing in the African American community and alongside the stories of two characters from the African American literary canon. I have argued that, like Helga Crane in *Quicksand* and Clare Kendry in *Passing*, Rahab is passing in Joshua 2. I arrived at this conclusion by exploring the history of passing, especially passing in the history of the African American community. I then offered a close reading of Joshua 2 that paid particular attention to Rahab's interaction with the other characters in the narrative. Finally, I connected the elements of passing with Rahab and her story.

In all of this exploration, the role of disconnection in the lives of the one who passes and her community members warrants attention as an aspect of Rahab's story. Allyson Hobbs speaks of passing as the anxious decision to break with a sense of communion in ways that upset the collective, "congregative character" of African American life.[31]

The disruption of the community collective must be particularly jarring. As Hobbs makes clear, passing meant many African Americans lived lives of exile because the choice to pass meant they no longer were connected to their communities of origin. Questions around what it may have been like for Rahab to disasscociate from her family remain. Was Rahab's break with her nuclear family (Rahab does not live under her father's roof as was customary in the culture) marked with emotional trauma, as was the case for Clare Kendry? How did members of Rahab's community of origin navigate societal boundaries if she chose to trangress these boundaries like Clare and Helga? Was movement in the sense of rarely settling down a part of Rahab's story as it was a part of Helga's? Did Rahab's relatives keep her secret by pretending not to know her in public spaces? At minimum, this chapter offers one solution to this disconnection for the reader. If disconnection plays a larger role in Rahab's narrative than the biblical text demonstrates, the experiences of literary figures like Clare Kendry and Helga Krane may function as connective creative fodder.

— 4 —

# REVEALING RAHAB
## A New Interpretive Strategy

## Introduction

The story of Rahab ends with the displaced Canaanite and her family, survivors of the destruction of Jericho, living out their days in the midst of the Israelites (Josh 6:25). Readers' unanswered questions about Rahab's "happily ever after" life among the Israelites are a subject that writers of the New Testament attempt to answer. Readers of the Gospel of Matthew learn that Rahab marries, has a son, and becomes the eventual great-great-grandmother of King David (Matt 1:1-6).[1] The writer of Hebrews comments on Rahab's personality and refers to her as a model of faith and obedience because "she had received the spies in peace" (Heb 11:31). Finally, the writer of James presents Rahab as one justified by her works because "she welcomed the messengers and sent them out by another road" (Jas 2:25). Taken together, these reports suggest that after the destruction of Jericho, the woman Rahab lived a full and exemplary life that may have been envied by Canaanites and Israelites alike.

Despite the commendable presentation of the "whore with a heart of gold," Rahab's story is suspicious.[2] It seems far-fetched that two men sent on a reconnaissance mission would gather enough data in a brothel to support a military raid. It is odd that the woman designated as "prostitute" in the text never engages in sexual intercourse in the narrative. Moreover, it is hard to believe a Canaanite would flourish among the people who burned down her or his city. Aside from the occasional daughter of a foreign king who married an Israelite king for political purposes, there are few examples of non-Israelite women flourishing among the Israelites. On the contrary, there are many stories of foreigners (especially foreign women) who suffered as Israelite captives.[3] Examples include the banishment of the Egyptian Hagar and her son from the home of Sarah and Abraham (Gen 16); the killing of the Midianite Cozbi by the Israelite priest Phinehas (Num 25); and the call for the expulsion of foreign women and children (Ezra 9–10). That Rahab would be the great-great-grandmother of King David is particularly questionable.

Perhaps the suspicious elements of Rahab's story are not dubious when the account is read not as her story, but as nationalistic Israelite propaganda. The story of Rahab, which begins in Joshua 2 and concludes in Joshua 6, is crafted in such a way that it persuades the reader that the god of the Israelites keeps promises. The story also presents the Israelites, as the people of YHWH, as promise keepers. This rhetoric is so effective that it eclipses an essential detail in the larger narrative of the Israelites' entry into the land promised to them by YHWH. In this chapter, I argue that the structural and organizational devices deployed in the story of Rahab conceal the important detail that the Israelites negotiate a treaty with a Canaanite in which the Canaanite assumes the position of the suzerain. Specifically, the preamble to the oath in Joshua 2:9-11 includes elements of an ancient Near Eastern suzerain treaty in which the Israelites are in the vassal position.

In what follows I examine the structural contours of Rahab's story meant to persuade the reader that YHWH is a promise keeper, and therefore will make good on the commitment to give the Israelites this land. I then turn to expose Rahab as a political power player, mapping the elements of an ancient Near Eastern treaty onto the elements of the oath negotiated between Rahab and the two men of Israel. I conclude this chapter with thoughts about how this reading of the text may inform a new interpretive strategy for modern readers. Please note that, in this chapter, I am not concerned with rabbinic references that attempt to read beyond the biblical text. Further, I accept the text in its final form and am not concerned with matters of dating, redaction, or textual criticism.

## Rhetoric to Establish YHWH as a Promise Keeper

### Structure

Ancient rhetoricians like the Roman philosopher Cicero divided their subject into five parts: invention (*inventio*), structure (*dispositio*), style (*elocutio*), memory (*memoria*), and delivery (*pronunciatio* or *actio*). [4] Whether the speaker's goal was intellectual (to teach), emotional (to touch an individual's feelings), or aesthetic (to hold another's rapt attention), rhetoricians carefully considered the arrangement of material when crafting their communication. Though developed at a different time and in a different culture than the composition of the Hexateuch,[5] Greco-Roman rhetorical models offer useful templates for understanding the Hebrew Scriptures. In the case of the biblical writer's treatment of Rahab's story, the chiastic structure of the text, in particular, is at the fore to persuade the reader that YHWH is a promise-keeping God.

A chiasm or chiasmus is a literary device in which words, clauses, or themes are laid out and then repeated but in inverted order. This creates an a-b-b-a pattern, or a "crossing" effect like the letter "x." A common variation on parallelism, this construction has a double effect by placing a more pronounced emphasis on the closely juxtaposed parts and by bracketing other parallel parts.[6] Chiasms appear throughout the Hebrew Bible. The description of Abraham's wealth in Gen 12:16 serves as an example of the basic A-B-C-C'-B'-A' construction of a chiasm:

> And he had sheep, oxen, (A)
> > male donkeys, (B)
> > > male [slaves] (C )
> > > and female slaves, (C')
> > female donkeys, (B')
> and camels. (A')

Rahab's story is part of the more expansive narrative arc that begins with YHWH promising land to Abraham (Gen 15), climaxes with Israel's entrance into Canaan, and resolves or ends with Abraham's descendants reaffirming their covenant in the new land (Josh 24). Structurally, the first portion of the Hexateuch, which includes the Abrahamic covenant, establishes YHWH as a promise maker, and YHWH's promise of land to the ancient Israelites is a significant theme of the Hexateuch. To that end, the second portion, which includes Israel's entrance into Canaan and conquest of Jericho, supports the claim that YHWH is a God who keeps promises. The third portion, which includes the Israelites reaffirming their covenant with YHWH, establishes Israel as beneficiaries of the promise. As the following graphic demonstrates, the chiastic structure of the text illumines the central focus on YHWH keeping YHWH's promise to the Israelites:

**A** YHWH makes a promise to Abraham/covenant about land (Gen 15:18)

   **B** Israel outside Canaan/the land; moving toward Canaan? (Gen–Josh 2:1a)

      **C** Pre-conquest (Josh 2:1b–6:20a)
         **1.** Israelite representatives inside Canaan
         **2.** Negotiation revolves around YHWH's claims: "I know"
         **3.** Israelite representatives outside Canaan (Josh 6:20a)

         **D** Israel in Canaan/possession of the land / YHWH's promise (Josh 6:20b)

      **C'** Post-conquest; loose ends (Josh 6:21-23)
         **1.** Canaanite representatives inside Rahab's home (Josh 6:23a)
         **2.** Israel fulfills negotiation commitment (Josh 6:23a)
         **3.** Canaanite representatives outside Rahab's home and outside Israel (Josh 6:23b)

   **B'** Canaan inside Israel/grafted into the community "until this day" [NRSV "ever since"]; expanding beyond Canaan? (Josh 6:25–Josh 23:16)

**A'** Abraham's descendants reaffirm promise made by YHWH/ renewal of covenant (Josh 24)

Telescoping to examine the pre-conquest, conquest, and post-conquest portions of the narrative illumines an interesting structural relationship between the pre-conquest (C) and post-conquest (C') portion of the narrative. To begin, readers find Israelite representatives are inside Canaan when the two men enter Rahab's home at the beginning of the pre-conquest portion of the narrative (Josh 2:1b–6:20a), and then find Canaanite representatives (Rahab, her father, her mother, her brothers, and all who belonged to her) inside Rahab's home at the beginning of the post-conquest portion of the narrative (Josh 6:21-23). Rahab's house has not changed—the *contents* of Rahab's house have changed.

In the pre-conquest portion of the narrative, Rahab begins her negotiation with the Israelites by stating, "I know that the LORD has given you the land" (2:9). After the Israelites root out Jericho, they fulfill the conditions of the negotiation by bringing all those found in Rahab's home out before the destruction of Jericho (Josh 6:23a). Again, Rahab's home is central to both portions of the narrative. Finally, from the moment Rahab lowers the two Israelite men down the side of the Jericho wall until they return and march around the wall of Jericho, Israel is outside Canaan (Josh 2:15–6:20a). Conversely, the Canaanites who were found in Rahab's house are placed outside Israel/the Israelite camp at the end of the post-conquest narrative (Josh 6:23b).

Structurally all of this "mirrored" activity happens on either side of the fulfillment of YHWH's promise: the conquest of Canaan.[7] In all of this, the idea of home is central. After wandering with no permanent home, the Israelites establish a home in Canaan. The writers emphasize the importance of the Israelites finding a home by bracketing the moment the Israelites move into their new home (via the conquest of Canaan) with references to being inside and outside of a home—in this case, Rahab's home. The mirror relationship between the pre- and post-conquest portions of the narrative focuses the reader's attention on the importance of home and the payout of a new home for the Israelites in Canaan.

## Style: Allusion and Repetition

The chiastic organization of the Hexateuch in general and the emphasis on home in the Rahab narrative in particular tune readers' focus on YHWH keeping YHWH's promise to the Israelites. While the biblical text's structure as a rhetorical tool connects the Israelites' entry into Canaan with the Abrahamic promise of land, the *style* (the rhetorical feature concerned with the choice of appropriate words and the use of figures and tropes) also attends to YHWH's commitment and character.[8] In Rahab's story, allusions and the repetition of words are the stylistic elements that point readers to YHWH as a promise keeper.

In Joshua 2, the allusions to Abraham's nephew Lot, the many references to Moses, and repetitious echoes of the Exodus experience remind the reader of YHWH's action in the world. These rhetorical devices predispose the reader to understand the conquest of Jericho as YHWH keeping the promise made to Abraham.

To begin, intertextual references to Abraham's nephew Lot connect the God of Joshua 2 to the God who made Abraham a promise in Genesis 15. In Joshua 2:3-4 the king's representatives inquire about the presence of foreigners, and Rahab explains that she does not know the origin of the foreign men. The king's messengers instruct Rahab to "Bring out [יצא, *ytza*] the men who have come to you, who entered your house, for they have come only to search out the whole land." Rahab responds by saying that she "did not know [ידע, *yda*] where they came from." This exchange between representatives of the community and a community outsider who is hosting visitors is an allusion to the story of Lot. In both narratives, the relationships between representatives of the community and an outsider and the acts of bringing out and of knowing are central.

In Genesis 19, the people of Sodom come to Lot's house and implore him to "Bring them [the foreigners] out." In Joshua 2, the representatives of the king want Rahab to "bring out" the foreigners. In both instances, the Hebrew verb *ytza* appears in the imperative form of what is called, in Hebrew grammar, the Hiphil stem. This imperative form moves the aspect of the verb from a simple causative action ("Make them come out") to one with a sense of urgency ("Bring them out!"). The representatives of the community at Sodom and of the king of Jericho are strongly demanding that Lot and Rahab, respectively, produce their houseguests.

Instead of acquiescing to the demand, Lot offers his daughters as an alternative. In Genesis 19:8 Lot responds, "Look, I have two daughters who have not known [*yda*] a man; let me bring them out to you."⁹ Similarly, in Joshua 2:4 Rahab offers an alternative truth when she says does not know [*yda*] the origin of the men in her house. Both Lot and Rahab speak of knowing or not knowing when responding to the demand to produce their houseguests.

In the Genesis and Joshua narratives, repetition reminds the reader of the history YHWH has with the Israelites in general and Abraham's family in particular. Readers are encouraged to anticipate that YHWH will protect those in Rahab's house in the same way YHWH protected those in Lot's house. Just as an act of divine intervention in the form of the heavenly messengers rendering the Sodomites blind and unable to attack Lot's house protected the visitors in Genesis 19, the divine (here invoked by Rahab during her negotiations beginning in Josh 2:9) protects those found under Rahab's roof in Joshua 6. As Rahab's story unfolds, YHWH ensures the survival of those found under her roof when the Israelites burn down the city of Jericho. The rhetorical device of allusion connects Rahab's story to that of Lot and persuades the reader to understand that YHWH keeps promises.

Secondly, Rahab's story deploys the rhetorical device of repetition to create a connection with the story of Moses. The most apparent connection between Rahab's story and Moses's narrative revolves around the dispatching of individuals to reconnoiter a foreign land. After escaping Egypt and leading the Israelites on their journey through the wilderness, Moses sends men to spy out the land of Canaan in Numbers 13:1-3. Similarly, Moses's successor, Joshua, sends two men as spies to "view the land, especially Jericho" in Joshua 2:1. A closer look at repetition and allusion between the two accounts unearths a shared spy narrative.[10] The story of the Israelites exploring Canaan under Moses's leadership (Num 13–14, Deut 1:19-46, and Josh 14:7-8) and the story of the Israelites surveying the new land with a view to their inheritances under Joshua's leadership (Josh 18–19) share at least five narrative elements. Each begins with (1) the selection or naming of the spies and moves to (2) the dispatching of the spies with specific instruction. The spies (3) report the execution of their mission, along with confirmation through an oracle or reference to the context of salvation history, before readers learn of (4) the return and the results. The event is followed by (5) a perfect tense formula confirming the gift of the land by YHWH before the matter concludes with (6) the action of entering or conquering the land.[11] When read together the similarities between the Moses story and the Joshua and Rahab story become clear.

Finally, in Joshua 2:9-11 Rahab rehearses the Exodus narrative from the perspective of one who has heard about YHWH's mighty acts. For Rahab, YHWH performed a miracle for the Israelites at the Red Sea and caused them to triumph over those who were in their way. Furthermore, these reports of YHWH's power have instilled fear in the hearts of the Canaanites, making Jericho an easy target for Israelite conquest. When Rahab concludes, "the LORD your God is indeed God" (Josh 2:11), she is echoing the words spoken by Moses in Deuteronomy: "the LORD is God" (Deut 4:39). This statement in Deuteronomy is part of Moses's recollection of God's mighty acts. In Joshua, Rahab speaks these words while rehearsing the mighty works of the Israelites' God. Rhetorically, the use of these words may encourage readers to understand Rahab as a Moses-like figure. Indeed, understanding Rahab as a new Moses is appropriate, as she eventually delivers her family from destruction in the same way Moses delivered his people from Egypt.[12]

While Moses plays an essential role in the deliverance of the Israelites, YHWH does the work of delivering the Israelites from Egyptian oppression. Similarly, even though Rahab says the two men will deliver her family, it is Rahab's statement of faith in YHWH that plays an essential role in the deliverance of her family. The use of repetition and allusion move the reader to understand YHWH as the one who delivers both the ancient Israelites and Rahab's family.

In summary, the chiastic structure of the Hexateuch, the repetition of certain words, and allusions to Moses and the Exodus experience—a defining event in the shared history of the Israelites—all conspire to persuade the reader of Rahab's story that YHWH makes and keeps promises, and a specific promise made to Abraham. This is the promise to provide the Israelites with land, which is fulfilled when the Israelites conquer Canaan at the conclusion of Rahab's story in Joshua 6. Moreover, not only do these rhetorical tools confirm YHWH's promise, but they also assure readers that YHWH and the Israelites are powerful and benevolent. YHWH is so powerful that even a marginalized foreign woman recognizes YHWH's supremacy. The foreign woman's understanding of YHWH as superior is apparent in her interaction with the two Israelite men (Josh 2:9-11). Reading with the text, the Israelites' benevolence is demonstrated when they spare the foreign woman and her family from destruction and allow them to live "in Israel ever since" (Josh 6:25). Additionally, not only did Rahab live among the Israelites, but she is celebrated as the great-great-grandmother of King David.[13] YHWH and the Israelites are, indeed, benevolent.

## Driving Ideology

Despite pointing the reader's attention in a particular positive direction, these rhetorical features and devices cannot camouflage what we see as horrific aspects of Rahab's story. The ideology that drives the narrative of Joshua, including the account of Rahab, affirms the destruction of a group of people. It affirms, in fact, that killing people in order to take ownership of land occupied by another is permissible and celebrated when YHWH promises the land. An ideological read of Rahab's story highlights how the work of othering the foreign Rahab persuades readers to accept the annihilation of the Canaanite community in service to YHWH fulfilling promises.[14]

The biblical writers send a clear message to indigenous people: when someone comes to take their land in the name of the invader's deity, the only option is to "be a Rahab, be a traitor to one's own people and side with the invaders—negotiate, join their religion, serve their god, and help them out."[15] Furthermore, this reading allows the interpreter to discern a threefold strategy for the destabilization of a people. The first strategy is the sexualization of the indigene as a legitimating of the dispossession and holocaust.[16] The writer of Joshua 2 does this immediately by introducing Rahab as a זנה (*zonah*) or prostitute. Although Rahab does not engage in any sexual activity in the text, the designation of *zonah* positions Rahab squarely as one engaged in the work of sex and figures her home as a brothel.

The second part of the destabilization strategy involves the cult or religion of the indigenes. Here, Randall C. Bailey points to the Deuteronomic Law Code (Deut 12:2-4), which sanctions the Israelites' destruction of shrines and cultic artifacts belonging to the conquered.[17] Another example of the destabilization program is found in Judges 1:11, which reads, "From there they went against the inhabitants of Debir (the name of Debir was formerly Kiriath-sepher)." Bailey argues that the writer's decision to transliterate the city name as *Kiriath-sepher* conceals the more accurate translation of the city name and masks its importance. The former city name is properly translated as "city of the book," which suggests Debir formerly housed a library. Misrepresenting Debir (formerly known as *Kiriath-sepher*) is an example of the destruction of the intellectual property of indigenous people, the third and final element of the destabilization strategy.[18] The writer of Joshua destabilizes the Canaanites and in effect legitimates their oppression by presenting Rahab (the only named Canaanite in this narrative) as a prostitute. Between Joshua 2 and 6 the Israelites murder a community, plunder its physical assets, and absorb a fraction of its people as the spoils of war. The readers are encouraged to overlook or read over these harmful elements of the story of the entry into Canaan.

The rhetorical features and devices detailed in this chapter aid the telling of an exciting story in the book of Joshua, even as they make it difficult to find horror in the story of the conquest. The rhetorical conventions deployed in the story of Rahab conceal not only the horror of what the Israelites do to the Canaanites, but also the critical detail that in this story the Canaanite woman negotiates a treaty with the Israelite men in which she adopts the position of the powerful suzerain.

## Rahab as a Dominant Suzerain

Many English translations of Joshua 2:14, 20, and 21 suggest that the two men are concerned with others finding out their "business," ostensibly their espionage on behalf of the Israelites.[19] Verse 14 reads, "The men said to her, 'Our life for yours! If you do not tell this business [*debir*] of ours, then we will deal kindly and faithfully with you when the LORD gives us the land.'" Verse 20 reads, "But if you tell this business [*debir*] of ours, then we shall be released from this oath that you made us swear to you." Verse 21 records Rahab's response: "According to your words [*debirim*], so be it." Although the same Hebrew noun *debir* is used in all three verses, English translators render the word differently: the two men speak of "their business" while Rahab confirms their "words."[20]

When translators put "business" in the mouths of the two men, the reader understands the issue to be their work of spying on behalf of the Israelites. As the plot of spying out the land unfolds, readers get caught up in worrying that exposure of the two spies' business of espionage will result in their death at the hands of the Canaanites. Readers get so caught up they read over the fact that, if the Hebrew term *debir* is translated as "word" throughout the verbal exchange, the issue for the spies is not being found behind enemy lines, but their literal *words*, the oath they have sworn with Rahab. A translation approach that translates *debir* as "word" throughout the exchange reveals a more significant problem for the Israelites: the representatives of the Israelites have entered into a treaty relationship with a Canaanite.

In the ancient world, a treaty was a binding agreement between political parties; a contract of sorts.[21] Nahash makes a treaty in 1 Samuel, kings Hiram and Solomon make a treaty in 1 Kings, Ephraim makes a treaty with Assyria in Hosea 12, and various nations make treaties in Joshua 9.[22] A treaty was often authorized or confirmed by an oath. An oath was a solemn promise that demonstrated the speaker's commitment and often ratified a treaty.

Referring to their agreement to spare her family in return for her protecting them from the king of Jericho's army, the spies add the stipulation that under certain circumstances they "will be released from this oath [*shevu'at*] that you have made us swear to you" (Josh 2:17). The Israelites want to be released from the agreement that was, in effect, a treaty between them and Rahab the Canaanite.[23] In the ancient world a treaty was a binding agreement between parties. Those parties were some combination of individuals and kings (as representatives of nations). In this instance, the treaty is between an individual and representatives of a nation, but these individuals are not equals. In this way, this agreement has all the markings of a suzerain treaty.

Two types of treaties were most prevalent in the ancient world: the parity treaty, in which the two parties are presumed equals, and the suzerain treaty, in which one party, the suzerain, is superior to the other, the vassal (a medieval term). In suzerain treaties the parties are not equal. These are treaties between a superior and an inferior, like those between various kings of Assyria and Babylon and kings of Israel and Judah. Several metaphors are used to describe the relationship of suzerain to vassal, including master-servant and father-son. Consider Hosea 12:1, in which the smaller group, Ephraim, becomes a vassal to Assyria, and Ezekiel 17:13, in which Jerusalem is the inferior to Babylon; these are examples of suzerainty treaties. The oath (a covenant, really) between the Israelites and Rahab has all the markings of a suzerain treaty.

Suzerain treaties usually included six (6) elements: (1) The preamble gives the identification of the suzerain and (2) a statement of the history of the relationship between the two groups. This history usually emphasizes the benevolent actions of the suzerain toward the vassal. (3) The third element of a suzerain treaty is stipulations. These are the obligations imposed upon the vassal, generally detailing the requirements of loyalty to the suzerain, including prohibition of relationships with other powers, prohibition of attacks on another vassal or the suzerain, requirements to respond to a call to assistance from the suzerain, requirement to submit disputes with another vassal to the suzerain, and payment of tribute. (4) Next, the treaty outlines provision for deposit of copies of the treaty in the temples of the principal gods of the two parties, and often for its periodic public reading. (5) The fifth element is the identification of a divine witness to the treaty. In ancient Near Eastern documents, this usually includes lengthy lists of national deities of both parties who are summoned as witnesses to the treaty. (6) A generic suzerain treaty concludes with blessings for observance of the treaty and curses for violations of it, to be carried out by the gods who were its ultimate guarantors.[24]

In the case of the treaty established in Joshua 2 between Rahab and the two Israelites, Rahab is positioned as the suzerain. Rahab introduces herself at the beginning of the negotiation sequence when she states, "I know" (Josh 2:9), thereby fulfilling the first element of a suzerain treaty. Rahab then reminds the Israelites of her experience with them when she states, "Now then, since I have dealt kindly with you" (Josh 2:12). This fulfills the second element of the suzerain treaty. Third, Rahab establishes stipulations that the Israelites will deal kindly with her family.[25] There are no provisions in this treaty, but the evidence of the red cord serves as the witness, the fifth element. In many ways, the inclusion of the red cord is a bargaining tool in the treaty negotiations. This stipulation frees the Israelites of their obligation should Rahab not meet this condition of their agreement. Instead of a list of deities to witness the treaty, the cord is the sign of the covenant.[26] The suzerain concludes the treaty with the statement, "According to your words" (Josh 2:21). Rahab's final statement is the final element of the treaty: the blessing.

The power dynamics in this passage are important. Power (German *Macht*) as understood by the social theorist Max Weber is instructive here. Weber understands power as the probability that one actor within a social relationship will be in a position to carry out his own will despite resistance.[27] In Weber's schema, there are two major types of power: *power-to-do* and *power-over*. *Power-to-do* is an ability, aptitude, or proficiency. Although power may be understood as *power-to-do*, as in the French verb *pouvoir*, the Weberian notion of power as *power-over* reflects power in Rahab's story. Biblical examples of *power-over* relationships include the relationships between kings and their subjects, or military leaders and their soldiers, as well as Sarah's exercising power over Hagar (Gen 16) and Jezebel's directing the actions of the elders and nobles in the matter of Naboth's vineyard (1 Kgs 21:5-16).[28] Rahab is in a power-over relationship with the Israelite spies.

In Joshua 2 Rahab assumes a more powerful position than the Israelite men. If the reader understands Rahab as a barmaid or innkeeper who would have maintained a semi-professional relationship with the court, her profession uniquely positioned her as an advisor to the king.[29] Rahab would have been obligated to inform the palace of recent arrivals within the gates of the city. In her interaction with the Israelite men, she begins already in a position of some authority that can leverage that political positioning in her favor. Her covenant was more than a personal "Hail Mary" to save herself from imminent destruction; this was a serious political agreement. Importantly, in this treaty-like engagement, Rahab is figured as the suzerain and the Israelite men as the vassals. Moreover, not only are the Israelite men beholden to a Canaanite, they are beholden to a Canaanite woman. In return for the promise of keeping their secret (whether it be the fact they made an oath with a foreigner or that they were in Canaan as spies), the Canaanite sovereign (interestingly, all this oath-making takes place in Canaanite territory) promises to ensure the immediate safety and protection of the Israelite vassals while/as they are in Canaanite territory (specifically, in Rahab's house in Jericho). The Israelites are the vassals because they are in the dependent position; at this point in the story, they need Rahab more than she needs them. Rahab is in the dominant sovereign position. Rahab is upsetting the status quo. This Canaanite woman is assuming roles traditionally left to Israelite men. Rahab is different. Rahab is a power player. Rahab acts as the ruler or the dominant suzerain.

To emphasize the importance of fidelity to the LORD only, in Exodus 23 the Israelites are instructed not to enter into covenant relationship with non-Israelites or their gods. While this admonition is most probably meant to guard against the Israelites being persuaded to oppose the LORD, this consideration informs the two Israelites' engagement with the foreigner Rahab in Joshua 2. This stipulation explains why, with the exception of political alliances between kings, there are few examples of Israelites entering into binding agreements with foreigners in the biblical text.[30]

In summary, during the negotiation portion of the narrative, the Hebrew word *debir* is used three times. While *debir* may be translated "word," "thing," "matter," or "business," many English translations choose to translate the word as "matter" or "business" when it is said by the two Israelite men and as "word" when Rahab says it. In these instances, the spies ask Rahab to conceal their business, and Rahab asks that things be according to their words. An interesting thing occurs when *debir* is translated consistently as "word." Here, the two Israelite men are concerned about Rahab concealing their words. The words are those spoken as part of articulating an oath. The Israelites are concerned, then, about making sure no one knows that they have entered into a binding agreement (an oath) with a foreign woman. Again, Israelites were not to enter into covenant relationship with anyone other than YHWH or the people of YHWH. Rahab reinforces the seriousness of the oath when she says, "according to your words," using the same Hebrew word.

The critical concern with this oath, the one that is masked by the use of "business" in verses 14 and 20, is that the Canaanite woman assumes the position of the suzerain in this negotiated treaty. The Israelite men did not want Rahab to disclose the fact they had entered into a treaty with a foreign woman in which they assumed the vassal position, because Israelites were not to make covenants with foreigners. The rhetoric of Joshua 2 as part of the conquest narrative lends itself to readers accepting the concern about the exposure of Israelite espionage. The rhetoric almost eclipses the broader concern of binding the Israelite community to a foreign woman via suzerain treaty. A close reading of the exchange between the Israelite men and the Canaanite woman exposes the fact that the two men do not want Rahab to tell anyone of their words—of their treaty.

## Conclusion

The book of Joshua in general and the story of Rahab in particular are works of propaganda that advance the idea that YHWH is a promise keeper. YHWH makes a promise to Abraham in Genesis 15 and makes good on that promise in Joshua 6 when the Israelites invade Canaan. Canonically, it is probably no coincidence that the promise is fulfilled at the end of the Hexateuch, before the introduction of the problematic entrance into and settlement of Canaan, a series of events full of contradictions.[31]

The Israelites burned down the Canaanite city of Jericho, absorbed anonymous survivors into their community, and remembered the incident as a pivotal event in the life of ancient Israel. The conquest is for the biblical writers an example of the fulfillment of YHWH's promise. The propaganda has worked so well that many modern readers overlook or read over an essential element of Joshua 2: the Israelites enter into an oath-treaty agreement with a Canaanite. The Canaanite-Israelite treaty is problematic because, as followers of YHWH, the Israelites were not to be in covenant relationship with anyone other than YHWH.

My reading of Rahab's story illumined rhetorical features and devices deployed in the story of Rahab to conceal some critical details in the conquest narrative. While it is clear the Israelites eventually establish themselves in the land promised by YHWH, the structure and organization of the narrative eclipses a less heroic element of the story. Attention to rhetoric provides a more balanced and less biased understanding of the events depicted in the text. Likewise, attention to rhetoric may benefit modern readers of texts beyond the Bible. Modern exegetes may unearth new insights should they examine the rhetoric of public historical documents, newspaper stories printed during tumultuous times in history, or transcripts of speeches made by famous people. Doing so may provide new insights into our understanding of history, which impacts the present and informs the future.

## 5

# RECONSIDERING RAHAB

Possibilities in the Midst of the Israelites

## Introduction

The writer of Joshua explains that after being spared by the Israelites, the Canaanite Rahab and her family "ha[ve] lived in Israel ever since" (Josh 6:25). This explanation presents Rahab's existence among the Israelites as routine, mundane, commonplace. At minimum, the relocation of Rahab and her Canaanite family is not a cause for the reader's concern. Reading imaginatively with the text, these Canaanites survive destruction of their city by the conquering Israelite army and ostensibly live out their days in peace among the Israelites. The careful reader might be suspicious of such a "happily ever after" ending. Such a neat end to such a messy story may hint at a tragedy that is jettisoned to the recesses of the larger story of the Israelites and their God.[1]

Readers of the Hebrew Bible are left with a series of unanswered questions about Rahab's life after the destruction of Jericho. These biblical writers do not mention Rahab (unlike other pivotal characters in the life of the Israelites) in any genealogy,[2] identify her among the Israelites in the stories of the monarchs, or resolve her narrative with a death notice. If anything, Rahab's story ends on an ominous note. Indeed, little is revealed about Rahab's life in the First Testament. The Matthean genealogy of Jesus includes Salmon and Rahab as the parents of Boaz, the great-grandfather of King David (Matt 1:5). This Boaz connection means Rahab is the great-great-grandmother of King David.[3] According to the writer of Hebrews, because she "received the spies in peace," Rahab is a model of faith and obedience (Heb 11:31). The writer of James presents Rahab as one justified by her works because she "welcomed the messengers and sent them out by another road" (Jas 2:25). Reading with the text, as a maternal ancestor of both King David and Jesus, Rahab seems to have lived a life to be envied by Canaanites and Israelites alike.

In this chapter, I suggest the references to Rahab living and ostensibly flourishing in the Israelite community are rhetorical devices meant to persuade the reader to accept the otherwise deplorable actions of the marauding Israelites despite the historical extrabiblical evidence, which suggests Canaanites like Rahab and her family were oppressed and lived poorly among the Israelites.[4] Readers are to believe all was well for Rahab. On the contrary, for Rahab and her family, to live among the Israelites meant to live in hostile territory. In what follows I consider what most probably happened to foreign men and women after conquest during biblical times. I approach the concern of Rahab "in the midst" by first attending to the Hebrew language deployed in her story and then considering the role ancient military practices may have played in Rahab's life. I begin by situating the Joshua text as the response to YHWH's *herem* or ban directive (the genocidal call for the utter and total destruction of an enemy) in Deuteronomy, and then consider connections between ancient warfare protocols and the action depicted in Joshua 6.[5] I conclude this chapter with a discussion of how foreigners (especially foreign women) most probably existed in the biblical world.[6] Importantly, I challenge the idea that Rahab could have seamlessly integrated into the Israelite community and lived a full and satisfying life.

## The Book of Joshua as a Response to YHWH's Directive

The beginning of the book of Deuteronomy details Moses's transition of leadership to Joshua and his instruction to Israel to keep the Torah. Upon their entry into the new land, the Israelites are to destroy the Hittites, Girgashites, Amorites, Canaanites, Perizzites, Hivites, and Jebusites. According to Deuteronomy 7:2, YHWH directs the Israelites to "utterly destroy" these nations, "make no covenant with them," and "show them no mercy." The Israelites are to commit genocide against the inhabitants of the land of promise.[7] Here we see that the Deuteronomistic Historian presents Israel's entry into Canaan as a response to a directive from YHWH such that the directive regarding the *herem* or ban given in Deuteronomy 7 is the basis for Joshua's activity as he leads Israel across the Jordan River to the land of promise. The connections between the *herem* and Joshua's actions are clear.

In response to the directive articulated in Deuteronomy 7, the book of Joshua details the Israelite entry and possession of Canaan, the land of promise. Based upon a positive report from the two men sent to spy on the land of Jericho, Joshua and the Israelites follow the priests as they carry the Ark of the Covenant across the Jordan River in a manner reminiscent of Moses crossing the Red Sea on dry land (Josh 3:1-17). The people camp at Gibeath-haaraloth. Then Joshua circumcises all the children of the warrior Israelites who had died in the wilderness (Josh 5:3), and the community celebrates the Passover before Joshua experiences a theophany in which a messenger of the LORD instructs him to "remove the sandals from your feet, for the place where you stand is holy" (Josh 5:10-15).

When the Israelites finally reach the Canaanite city of Jericho, they march around the city seven times while the priests blow trumpets and "the wall fell down flat; so the people charged straight ahead into the city and captured it" (Josh 6:20). In the midst of the fury of conquest activity, Joshua instructs the two who had spied out the land to retrieve Rahab and those with her (Josh 6:22-23). The Israelites burn down the city of Jericho and, according to the biblical narrator, Rahab and her family "ha[ve] lived in Israel ever since" (Josh 6:25).

The overarching concern of the Joshua narrative is the Israelites' entry into the Canaanite city of Jericho. Allusions to Abraham and Moses present the Israelite entry into Canaan as divinely sanctioned. Joshua's mass circumcision of the Israelites at Gibeath-haaraloth (Josh 5:3) harkens back to the Abrahamic covenant in Genesis 17:10, and Joshua's leadership while the Israelites keep Passover at Gilgal (Josh 5:10) echoes the cultic meal instituted under Moses's leadership in Exodus 12. Importantly, Joshua's encounter with the commander of the army of the LORD while near Jericho (Josh 5:13-15) reminds the reader of Moses's theophoric encounter with the burning bush in Exodus 3:1-6. Consequently, the conquest of the Canaanites seems to follow the divine directive of genocide found in Deuteronomy.

When careful readers ask questions about the treatment of Rahab living "in Israel ever since," they cannot help querying potential danger for Rahab. Readers are told the Canaanite Rahab exists "in Israel," but this curt addendum to the Canaanite woman's story does not convey the potential danger of a foreigner in biblical Israel.

## Canaanites "in the midst" of Israelites

English translators treat this Joshua 6:25 passage variously. For example, the King James Version renders the Hebrew phrase as "she dwelleth in Israel even unto this day," the New International Version reads, "she lives among the Israelites to this day," and the New Revised Standard Version interprets the passage as "Her family has lived in Israel ever since." Each of these English translations leaves the reader with the idea that Rahab and her family nicely settled among the Israelites. Perhaps the popular modern paraphrase *The Message* works the hardest to read in favor of the Israelites: "She is still alive and well in Israel." None of these English translations hint at any discord or danger for Rahab or members of her family.

Found most often in the writings of the Deuteronomistic Historian (DH), the Hebrew phrase *wa teshev be qerev* ("they dwelt in the midst of") accompanies stories of warfare and is not unique to the Joshua 6 conquest narrative. For example, when the Israelites do not drive out the Geshurites or the Maacathites, "Geshur and Maacath live in the midst of Israel [*be qerev yisra'el*]" (Josh 13:13). When the Israelites do not drive out the Canaanites who live in Gezer, the Canaanites live in the midst of (*be qerev*) Ephraim (Josh 16:10) but are made to perform forced labor.[8] The Asherites (also Israelites) live in the midst of (*be qerev*) the Canaanites, and Naphtali lives in the midst of (*be qerev*) the Canaanites (Judg 1:32-33).

Finally, the writer summarizes the relationship between Israel and inhabitants of the lands they conquered thus: "So the Israelites dwelt among the Canaanites, the Hittites, the Amorites, the Perizzites, the Hivites, and the Jebusites" (Judg 3:5 NKJV). As these examples demonstrate, the Hebrew phrase *wa yeshev ba qerev yisra'el* ("and they dwelt in the midst of the Israelites") is used when the Israelites engage in warfare. The wartime context of the phrase *be qerev*, therefore, warrants an examination. Relevant to Rahab's story, this examination must consider how the ancients treated human spoils of war.

## A Word about Ancient Warfare

Ancient military practices, the treatment of non-Israelites as spoils of war, and the treatment of female prisoners of war in ancient times all inform a nuanced understanding of what it may have meant for Rahab and her family to live in the midst of Israel. The ancient Israelites' approach to war and war-making emerges from the context of warfare practices in the broader ancient world. In his article "Prisoners of War in Early Mesopotamia," Ignance Gelb considers the characteristics and social statuses of ancient prisoners of war (POWs). Generally, POWs were considered part of the spoils of war—human booty—and were completely at the mercy of their captors.

POWs could be slain on the battlefield or sacrificed later in the temples. POWs could be assigned to work for the palace or given to the temples. As human booty, kings and nobles could be kept for ransom or as hostages. In sum, as POWs individuals could be sold, given away, or set free.[9] The existence and treatment of POWs in ancient Israel contextualizes the activity in the Hebrew Bible. The ancient Israelites most probably followed similar practices in the treatment of their POWs.

## Warfare in the Biblical World

War is a major concern of the biblical text in general, and the historical books in particular. The action depicted in the text transpires during historical periods in which Egyptian, Assyrian, and Babylonian empires waged war to establish dominance in the Levant. Under the leadership of both Moses and Joshua, Israel engaged in war during their journey to the Promised Land.[10] When judges ruled, the Israelites fought Canaanites, Midianites, Ammonites, and Philistines.[11] During the time of the monarchy, Saul and David each led war efforts against the Ammonites (1 Sam 11; 2 Sam 10), Philistines (1 Sam 13–14; 17; 31; 2 Sam 5 and 21), Amalekites (1 Sam 15 and 30), Arameans (2 Sam 10), and various individuals.[12] Finally, the biblical text records the Northern Kingdom fighting Assyria (2 Kgs 15–17) and the Southern Kingdom battling the Egyptians (1 Kgs 14), Assyria (2 Chr 32 and 33), and Babylon (2 Kgs 24–25).

One consequence of war is the confiscation of goods from a defeated enemy.[13] The spoils of war, these confiscated goods, could be material items, livestock, or human beings. Jewelry is part of the booty in Judges 8; clothing is part of the booty in 2 Chronicles 20; and David divides the booty among his warriors in 1 Samuel 30. Sheep, goats, and camels are part of the spoils of war in 2 Chronicles 14; and mention is made of the booty as both animal and human in Numbers 31. The biblical record, however, is not consistent in its portrayal of the treatment of human lives as booty. The writer of Deuteronomy 20 speaks of destroying human spoils of war and of enslaving persons as part of booty (vv. 14 and 16).

The Israelites engaged in war and, as with any war, the victors took prisoners as part of the booty. Some human booty or prisoners of war (POWs) were killed and the lives of others were spared. For example, the Babylonian King Nebuchadnezzar killed Israelite priests and other community leaders (2 Kgs 25:18-21), and the king of Israel killed the king of Judah (2 Chr 28:5). Some war victims were slain on the battlefield: the Israelites killed the kings, warriors, and non-virgin women in the war against the Midianites (Num 31). Similarly, the men of Ai killed Israelites on the slope outside the gate of Ai (Josh 7:5) before the Israelites defeated Ai in an ambush outside the city (Josh 8:19-29). Conversely, the biblical record demonstrates that not all POWs were killed. As an example, kings and nobles were kept or confined in prisons as ransom or as hostages. King Hoshea (2 Kgs 17:4) and King Manasseh were taken away in shackles by the king of Assyria (2 Chr 33:11).

Motives other than political dominance undergirded war efforts in the biblical world, and these motives had far-reaching implications. Although Israel fought wars to acquire food or land, preserve itself in the face of threat, conquer, and escape from having been conquered, the biblical writers interpreted warfare theologically.[14] This theology frames biblical war as holy war. The narrative beginnings of Israel as a nation and the Exodus experience of the Israelites are examples of this theological framing of biblical war. Here, YHWH is a "man of war" (Exod 15:3 KJV), and the "LORD of Hosts," which could, and perhaps should, be translated, "supreme leader of armies."[15] God is intimately involved in Israel's war activities, and the references to the LORD's *herem* directive in Deuteronomy, the many theophanies, and the Israelites' particular cultic activities frame Joshua's invasion of Jericho as a holy war. In fact the biblical account of the Israelite entrance into Canaan has all the markers of holy war.

The LORD instructs Joshua about the military campaign

beginning in the first chapter of Joshua. As the Israelites prepare to cross the Jordan River, the LORD assures Joshua that "no one shall be able to stand" against them as they move to possess the vast promised land (1:5). The LORD promises to give the Israelites the land "from the wilderness and the Lebanon as far as the great river, the river Euphrates, all the land of the Hittites, to the Great Sea in the west shall be your territory" (Josh 1:4). While the LORD's directives say that no one will be able to stand against them, this anticipates the reality that the act of possessing the land will be met with conflict. The mention of warriors in Joshua 1:14 and the warning that those who rebel against the Israelites will die anticipates bloodshed as a consequence of the land's possession (Josh 1:14-18). Additionally, the language used to describe the Canaanites' response to the Israelites (i.e., "panic stricken" [NEB] or "melting in fear" [NIV] in Josh 2:24) presupposes the institution or ideology of holy war.[16] Therefore the continued presence of the foreigners in Israelite territory is problematic for the biblical writers and their understanding of God's promise of land rights.

According to Deuteronomy, the Israelites were under divine command to totally annihilate the inhabitants of the land.[17] That Israelites' enemies could continue to dwell in their midst reflects negatively upon the Israelites, because the enemies' continued presence signals that the Israelites have not fulfilled their duty as followers of YHWH. The presence of the enemy in the land supposedly given to the Israelites by their God does not comport theologically with the idea of YHWH as all-powerful.

The idea that YHWH is unable to deliver on the promise of conquest and land rights is a theological problem for the ancient Israelites. In many ways, Joshua 2 and 6 (with the inclusion of ban language in 6:21) establish the duty of the Israelites to drive out or exterminate the native inhabitants of Canaan. One way to resolve the problem of the continued presence of non-Israelites in the promised land is by pointing to Joshua 23:5, which avers that the LORD will push or drive out the remaining inhabitants of the land as long as Israel remains faithful to the covenant. That the annihilation is incomplete is a testament to the shortcomings of the Israelites and not an indictment upon their God.[18]

Despite many modern interpreters' efforts to soften the activity found in Joshua 6 by referring to it as a conquest, readers should understand Joshua as a text about war.[19] The conquest language can be misleading, because it is freighted with the idea that those who conquer are on the side of right and those conquered deserve—and are even made better because of—the conquest. To that end, conquest is often presented as the opposite of conflict: the attempt to bring order out of chaos.[20] For modern readers who have not lived through having their community overtaken by a foreign army, the concept of conquest seems innocuous, perhaps something that was done "back in the old days." However, conquest is synonymous with warfare, something very much prevalent in our own world.

The entire book of Joshua contains stories to support the theme of holy war. The purpose of the holy war is to take possession of the land, which YHWH promised to the patriarchs (Deut 1:8; 6:10, 18; 7:8; 34:4).[21] Chapters 1–11 of Joshua contain four full-length statements of the holy war theme: the conquest of Jericho, the second attack on Ai, and the Judean and Galilean campaigns.[22] These narratives stress that it is YHWH who takes the initiative in the conduct of the war, sends Israel into battle, and ensures its success. Moreover, divine intervention is implicit in the sudden collapse of the walls of Jericho.[23]

An important marker of holy war is the ratification of warfare in a theophoric manner. In Joshua's case, beginning in Joshua 1:1, the LORD instructs him to cross the Jordan River to take the land promised to the Israelites. Beginning in Joshua 5:13, in an episode reminiscent of Moses's burning-bush encounter, the "commander of the army of the LORD" instructs Joshua to remove the sandals from his feet, because he is standing on holy ground. The LORD then encourages Joshua to march around Jericho with priests for six days before the wall of the city falls. Finally, the LORD speaks directly to Joshua, tells him of the coming victory over Jericho, and provides instructions for the conquest beginning in Joshua 6:2. The encounter with the commander of the LORD's army who appears to Joshua with a drawn sword in his hand (5:13-15) is an example of the editor of the book of Joshua pointing to Joshua as Moses's true successor.[24]

In addition to the inclusion of theophoric direction and ratification, holy war is marked by extreme commitment on the part of its warriors. The type of sacrifice displayed by the warriors of Israel approaches religious fanaticism. As an example, the biblical writers describe warriors as single-minded in their commitment to war (Deut 20:5-9). Only warriors who looked upon engaging in combat as sacrifice could participate in war.[25] In the Joshua narrative, Israel's warriors participate in the ritual of circumcision before they begin the campaign against Jericho (Josh 5:2). Circumcision was a defining mark of covenant relationship between Israel and YHWH. Notably, the seven-day wait before taking Jericho may be a nod to the seven days of creation in Genesis. In each of these markers of holy war, the theological purposes read into the conduct of biblical war are intended to serve God and the goals of God.[26]

In sum, beginning in the fifth chapter of the book of Joshua, the writer makes it clear that the Israelites are engaging in warfare.

The use of "warriors" to describe Israelite males (Josh 5:4) and the mention of "armed men" following the priests into Jericho (Josh 6:13) are war language, the ritual of circumcision is not simply a cultic sign of covenant but a ritual act of preparation for war, and Joshua's theophany (Josh 5:13–6:5) includes instruction to take the city of Jericho. Importantly, the Canaanite city is "devoted to the LORD for destruction," and the people are to charge the city and capture it "by the edge of the sword" (6:17, 21). Jericho is massacred. The Israelites massacre the inhabitants of Jericho and burn down the city, as was the customary practice of the ancient world.[27]

### Foreign Women as Spoils of War

Concerns around foreign women as spoils of war or POWs are germane to a treatment of Rahab among the Israelites.[28] One way to make meaning out of the text is to understand that the biblical writers use Rahab to send the message to foreigners that the only way to save oneself and remain intact is to be a traitor to one's own people and side with the invaders—negotiate, join their religion, serve their god, and help them out.[29] Another interpretive approach concludes that those treatments of Rahab's story are insufficient that allow readers to reimagine Rahab as a "wise, sexually and economically independent woman" but do not recognize Rahab's hybridity as both an Israelite and a Canaanite.[30]

Still another perspective juxtaposes the Joshua conquest narrative with American origin stories and identifies the role of the indigenous helper in the four stages of the "myth of the empty land" motif. This way of reading highlights Rahab (like Sacagawea in American lore) as the exemplary foreign helper and literary pivot upon which land ownership shifts to the conquering nation as she sides with the invading people.[31] None of these interpretive paths adequately attends to Rahab as a Canaanite living among the Israelites. English translations of Rahab living "in Israel" and the narrative image of Rahab looking on at Jericho as it lies in ruins hold irony as she eventually gives birth to an Israelite child whose descendant—David and, later, Jesus—becomes the savior of his people. Yet there must have been immediate danger for Rahab.

The danger lies in the reality that women and children of overthrown nations often became slave property of the crown or the state and, as such, were abused and exploited in the ancient world.[32] There was a difference between the treatment of dependent women (slaves and serfs) and independent women (wives of rulers and ladies of the court).[33] Moreover, female POWs could be taken in marriage.[34]

The Bible addresses women as war captives in particular ways. To begin, in Numbers, Israelites take women of Midian and their children captive; Moses is upset that the women will be allowed to live; Moses orders the killing of children and "every woman who has known a man by sleeping with him." Israelites could keep young girls "who have not known a man" for themselves (Num 31:9, 15, 17-18). Additionally, Deuteronomy 21–25 details how women prisoners of war should be treated. In Deuteronomy, beautiful women are taken into Israelite homes where they shave their heads, cut their nails, and throw away their clothing and spend a month in mourning. After her month of mourning, the Israelite male may "go into" the woman. If the Israelite male is unsatisfied with the captive woman, he may release her but not sell her or treat her like a slave (Deut 21:10-14). These directives regarding foreign female POWs make the story of the Midianite Cozbi (Num 25) all the more interesting. This may be the treatment Cozbi experienced before she was murdered by the Israelite priest Phinehas.[35]

If one follows the *herem* directive laid out in Deuteronomy, the Canaanite Rahab should never have been spared or married into an Israelite family.[36] If Rahab was not married to the Israelite Salmon, she was most probably treated as a female prisoner of war. This prisoner-of-war status would have entailed a pregnancy as the result of what modern readers would understand as sexual abuse. To understand Rahab's pregnancy as sexual abuse and not the result of normative marital sexual relations undoubtedly challenges romantic readings of Rahab's story and complicates the genealogy of King David.

The suggestion that Rahab had a full life with the Israelites is debatable. So much of the story of the Hebrew Bible is about the Israelites establishing themselves as special, unique, different, and better than the other communities and cultures around them, that it seems dubious that a non-Israelite would find it easy to live among them. Furthermore, there are precious few examples in the biblical text of foreigners who lived robust lives and rose to prominence in the Israelite community. On the contrary, there are many stories of foreigners—especially foreign women—who suffered when they lived among the Israelites. Ezra exemplifies this treatment of foreign women when he tells the postexilic Israelites, "You have trespassed and married foreign women, and so increased the guilt of Israel" (Ezra 10:10).[37] To that end, both Ezra and Nehemiah frame marriages to foreign women as acts of such social and religious disobedience that the men are to separate themselves from their foreign wives and children (Ezra 10:44 and Neh 13).

The rhetoric of "she lived among the Israelites" eclipses the most probable scenario—Rahab was a prisoner of war. The existence of an "other" living among the Israelites was not peaceful. As a female prisoner of war, Rahab was probably sexually violated by the Israelite Salmon. The product of the non-consensual sexual encounter between Salmon and Rahab was Boaz, who was the great-grandfather of King David. This understanding of the genealogy of King David challenges romanticized readings of Rahab's story that frame her as the autonomous foremother of David and, by extension, Jesus.

## Conclusion

A nuanced understanding of the Hebrew phrase "they dwelt in the midst of Israel" expands the possibility that life for Rahab may have been uncomfortable among the Israelites. The wartime context of the phrase "they dwelt in the midst of" underscores that Rahab's story takes place in the midst of combat and conflict. Additionally, bringing information about military protocols to bear on the text—especially those protocols associated with female prisoners of war—highlights the possibility that Rahab did not simply integrate into the Israelite community.

The textual record suggests Rahab was most likely forced into marriage relations with Salmon, and their child was the result of forced sexual relations between an Israelite male and a foreign POW. For modern readers sensitive to women, their rights, and their bodily autonomy, this sort of revelation is shocking. To think the lineage of King David and of Jesus included unwanted sexual advances—indeed, sexual abuse—is daunting. By focusing the reader's attention on the spectacle of the Israelite conquest, the writers eclipse what can only have been the deplorable treatment of Rahab as a non-Israelite woman in Israelite territory.

The Bible's story often turns on unexpected people who drive the plot. Those who are rich and powerful are often and surprisingly upended, for example, by younger sons, nomadic wanderers, and foreign women. Who was Rahab? What was she? What happened to her? This much we know: she is an intriguing character whose story is layered with important concerns for modern readers. Despite—or perhaps precisely because of—her marginalized position, a careful reread of Rahab's story can prompt us to ask needed questions about identity, autonomy, difference, and privilege.

# ENDNOTES

## Introduction

1 According to the band's website, *Rahab* juxtaposes worldly fantasies with biblical realities by showcasing the fruitlessness of fear and the power of faith. *Rahab* includes songs such as "Reign," "Avarice," "Heathen Heart," "Allure," and "By Faith." For more information on Earth Groans visit http://www.earthgroans.com/bio.html. Additionally, the Moroccan DJ and producer Fadil El Ghoul may have borrowed a loose transliteration of the biblical monster Rahab for the spelling of his stage name, R3HAB.

2 Liz Curtis Higgs, *Bad Girls of the Bible: And What We Can Learn from Them* (Colorado Springs, CO: WaterBrook Press, 2013); Kasey van Norman, *Rahab: Don't Judge Me, God Says I'm Qualified*, Known by Name (Grand Rapids: Zondervan, 2018); and Jill Eileen Smith, *The Crimson Cord: Rahab's Story* (Grand Rapids: Fleming H. Revell Company, 2015).

3 Otto Eissfeldt found three literary sources, while Eckart Otto reduced this to two. See Otto Eissfeldt, *The Old Testament: An Introduction, Including the Apocrypha and Pseudepigrapha, and Also the Works of Similar Type from Qumran: The History of the Formation of the Old Testament*, trans. Peter R. Ackroyd (New York: Harper and Row, 1965), 252–53; and Eckart Otto, *Das Mazzotfest in Gilgal* (Stuttgart: W. Kohlhammer, 1975), 84–86.

4 Trent C. Butler, *Joshua*, Word Biblical Commentary 7 (Grand Rapids: Zondervan, 1983), 66.

5 Jan Dus and Hans-Joachim Kraus seek to reconstruct a cultic ritual that gave rise to the tradition, while Jay Wilcoxen has opted for three slightly different forms of cultic ritual as the basis for the story. See Jan Dus, "Die Analyse Zweier Ladeerzählungen Des Josuabuches (Jos 3-4 Und 6)," *Zeitschrift Für Die Alttestamentliche Wissenschaft* 72, no. 2 (1960), 119–20; Hans-Joachim Kraus, *Gottesdienst in Israel: Grundriss einer Geschichte des alttestamentlichen Gottesdienstes* (Munich: Chr

Kaiser, 1962), 187–89; and Jay Wilcoxen, "Narrative Structure and Cult Legend: A Study of Joshua 1-6," in *Transitions in Biblical Scholarship*, ed. Gösta W. Ahlström and John Coert Rylaarsdam (Chicago: University of Chicago Press, 1968), 52–53.

6 Avraham Lorberbaum Dafna, "Did the Wall of Jericho Collapse or Did the City Surrender?" *Jewish Bible Quarterly* 38, no. 1 (2010): 36. William F. Albright, Kathleen Kenyon, and others consider the collapse of the wall based upon dating the destruction as well as which wall (inner or outer) was destroyed.

7 Eugene H. Merrill, "The Conquest of Jericho: A Narrative Paradigm for Theocratic Policy?" *Bibliotheca Sacra* 169 (July–Sept 2012): 314.

8 Yahweh is the name of God that was revealed to Moses. It is often represented in biblical literature as *YHWH*, also called the tetragrammaton.

9 See Ruth 4:21. First Chronicles 2:11 renders a variant spelling of Salmon, Salma. See Kirk E. Lowery, "Salmon (Person)," *ABD* 5:906.

10 Additionally, the writer of Heb 11:31 lists the prostitute Rahab among the faithful, and she is held up as an example of justification by works in Jas 2:25.

# Chapter I

1 For more on the use of *zonah* in the Hebrew Bible, see Isabelle Hamley, "What's Wrong with 'Playing the Harlot'? The Meaning of זנה in Judges 19:2," *TynBul* 66, no. 1 (2015): 41–62.

2 Of the surveys distributed, twenty-four (24) were completed fully by women attending the Spiritual Transformation Conference of the 4th Episcopal District of the African Methodist Episcopal Church in Oak Brook, IL, in March 2019. Surveys reflected diversity among adult AMEC women over thirty years old as respondents included a mixture of ordained clergywomen and non-clergy/lay members. For the survey question and survey results, see Chart 2 at the end of this chapter.

3 Avaren Ipsen, *Sex Working and the Bible* (New York: Routledge, 2014), 4. Ipsen facilitated a reading group of activist sex workers who were all involved with the effort to decriminalize prostitution in Berkeley, CA: The Sex Worker Outreach Project (SWOP). The SWOP group read the stories of Rahab (Josh 2 and 6), the story of the two prostitutes and Solomon (1 Kgs 3:16-28), the anointing-woman traditions of John and the synoptic Gospels (John 12:1-8/Mark 14:3-9/Matt 26:6-13/Luke 7:36-50), and the apocalyptic visions of the whore of Babylon (Rev 17–19), prioritizing the SWOP women's subcultural knowledge of prostitution as a way to exegete biblical prostitution (Ipsen, 9). In this one-of-a-kind study, Ipsen compares feminist and liberation readings to some of the SWOP insights to show how a sex worker's standpoint can "crack open the texts in a new way" (12).

4 Ipsen, *Sex Working*, 74.

5 Ipsen, 74.

6 *Tanak(h)* is an acronym of the first Hebrew letter of each of the Masoretic text's three traditional divisions: Torah (teaching), Nevi'im (Prophets), and Ketuvim (Writings).

7 This reference is found in verse 18 in English translations, but in verse 19 in Hebrew manuscripts. The earnings of both a *zonah* and a male prostitute are abhorrent to the Lord. Here, the Hebrew word כלב (*kelev*, dog) is used to describe the male prostitute instead of some version of *zonah*. While both *zonah* and *kelev* are designations for individuals held in contempt by the Israelite community, many English translators render the noun *kelev* as "male temple prostitute" instead of "dog" or some other derogative descriptor. By introducing the term "prostitute," these translators weigh *kelev* with sexualized language.

8 Joseph Fleishman, *Father-Daughter Relations in Biblical Law* (Bethesda, MD: CDL Press, 2011), 223. As I note in *Daughters in the Hebrew Bible*, Fleishman misses the reality that in patriarchal societies, the legal codes protect the concerns of the male. An unmarried woman could not give consent because she did not have the legal authority to do so, and the concerns and legal standing of an unmarried female member of an Israelite household were tenuous at best. Fleishman himself explains that the purpose of the Lev 19 law is to prevent the proliferation of prostitution and its morally degrading effects on the Israelite community. See Kimberly D. Russaw, *Daughters in the Hebrew Bible* (Lanham, MD: Lexington Books/Fortress Academic, 2018), 12.

9 In the Hebrew canon the Prophets are divided into (1) the Former Prophets (Joshua, Judges, Samuel, and Kings) and (2) the Latter Prophets (Isaiah, Jeremiah, Ezekiel, and the Twelve, or Minor, Prophets: Hosea, Joel, Amos, Obadiah, Jonah, Micah, Nahum, Habakkuk, Zephaniah, Haggai, Zechariah, and Malachi).

10 Josh 2:1; 6:17, 22, 25; Judg 11:1; 16:1; 1 Kgs 3:16; 22:38.

11 Phyllis Trible, *Texts of Terror: Literary-Feminist Readings of Biblical Narratives* (Philadelphia: Fortress, 1984), 94.

12 The angel of the Lord instructs Samson's pregnant mother that her son will be a Nazirite to God from birth in Judg 13:5.

13 J. Cheryl Exum, "The Theological Dimension of the Samson Saga," *VT* 33, no. 1 (1983): 31. For more on the Nazirite vow see James L. Crenshaw, *Samson: A Secret Betrayed, A Vow Ignored* (Atlanta: John Knox, 1978); and Joseph Blenkinsopp, "Structure and Style in Judges 13-16," *JBL* 82, no. 1 (1963): 65–76.

14 Renita J. Weems, *Battered Love: Marriage, Sex, and Violence in the Hebrew Prophets* (Minneapolis: Fortress, 1995), 16. Each of these relationships operated within a system that had rules of power and punishment. According to the system, one party (that is, master or parent) exercised power over the other party (that is, slave or child). Importantly, the subordinate—not the authority—was obligated to maintain this power dynamic. It was the slave's responsibility to be productive in his or her labor and obedient to the master. If the subordinate did not fulfill her or his role, the authority figure was obligated to punish the subordinate. For example, if a slave did not produce or was disobedient, the master was obligated to punish the slave. This presentation of the power dynamics between the authority figure and the subordinate predisposed the hearer to empathize with the authority figure when punishment—regardless of how harsh—was meted out. In the biblical world of the prophets, God was obligated to punish Israel because

Israel did not fulfill its role as subordinate. Weems notes that, in this world of fixed power relations, it is not surprising that God was always masculinized as the husband and Israel was always feminized as the wife (*Battered Love*, 18).

15  Weems, 17–18.

16  John D. W. Watts, *Isaiah 1–33* (Grand Rapids: Zondervan, 1985), 38. For more on Isa 1 see Douglas R. Jones, "Exposition of Isaiah Chapter One Verses Twenty-One to the End," *SJT* 21, no. 3 (1968): 320–29.

17  Thomas Renz, "Proclaiming the Future: History and Theology in Prophecies against Tyre," *TynBul* 51, no. 1 (2000): 30.

18  Mark Leuchter, whose project interrogates the dating of the Isa 23 text, suggests the writer of First Isaiah deploys the rhetoric of *zonah* in ways that would have demanded attention from and commanded authority over the prophet's audience. See Mark Leuchter, "Tyre's 70 Years," *Bib* 87, no. 3 (2006): 417.

19  Weems, *Battered Love*, 18–19.

20  Weems, 30.

21  Weems, 28.

22  Weems, 29.

23  The mixed gender roles are interesting here.

24  Weems, *Battered Love*, 52.

25  Weems, 58.

26  The understanding of women as victims of rape is anachronistic for the ancient Israelites. Unauthorized sexual interaction with a woman who was under the authoritative gaze of another male (that is, her father, her husband, or her brother) was a transgression against the *male*. The father, husband, or brother—not the woman—was considered the victim.

27  Jerusalem is the *zonah* who dishonors her husband, misconstrues his generosity for weakness, and underestimates his power over her as his wife. See Weems, *Battered Love*, 64.

28  Andrew Sloane, "Aberrant Textuality? The Case of Ezekiel the (Porno) Prophet," *TynBul* 59, no. 1 (2008): 53–76. Also see Athalya Brenner and Fokkelien van Dijk-Hemmes, *On Gendering Texts: Female and Male Voices in the Hebrew Bible* (Leiden: Brill, 1996); Athalya Brenner, *The Intercourse of Knowledge: On Gendering Desire and 'Sexuality' in the Hebrew Bible* (Leiden: Brill, 1997); Athalya Brenner, "On Prophetic Propaganda and the Politics of 'Love': The Case of Jeremiah," in *A Feminist Companion to the Latter Prophets,* ed. A. Brenner (Sheffield, UK: Sheffield Academic, 1995), 256–74; and Robert Carroll, "Whorusalamin: A Tale of Three Cities as Three Sisters," in *On Reading Prophetic Texts,* ed. Bob Becking and M. Dijkstra (Leiden: Brill, 1996), 67–82.

29  Brenner and van Dijk-Hemmes, *Gendering Texts*, 175. Oholah and Oholibah (KJV: Aholah and Aholibah) are allegorical names given to the Northern and Southern Kingdoms. See J. T. Whitney, "Oholibamah, Oholah, Oholibah," *NBD,* 843.

30 Brenner and van Dijk-Hemmes, *Gendering Texts*, 172–73. Van Dijk-Hemmes eventually concludes Israel's sin in Egypt actually consisted of its being oppressed, and that such a statement's lack of logic can be made acceptable by the transformation of a people into metaphorical women (173).

31 Weems, *Battered Love*, 62.

32 Douglas Stuart, *Hosea–Jonah* Word Biblical Commentary 31 (Grand Rapids: Zondervan, 1987), 267.

33 The Hebrew verb *znh* appears as Qal imperfect 3fp.

34 This reference is found in Joel 3:3 in English translations, but in Joel 4:3 in Hebrew manuscripts.

35 The Hebrew word *'ishah* means "woman" or "wife."

36 Because there are no instances of *'ish zonah* (man/husband of whoredom) it seems redundant to require the modifier *'ishah* (woman of) for the noun *zonah*. Every *zonah* in the biblical world is a woman.

37 Stuart notes *zonunim* "prostitution" is an abstract noun, built on the plural pattern frequently used for abstracts as an alternative to the feminine singular. The term *'eshet zenunim*, wife/woman of whoredom, can hardly mean "prostitute" (*zonah*), and "woman/wife of prostitution" is awkward in English. See Stuart, *Hosea–Jonah*, 23.

38 For treatments of sacred or cultic prostitution see Stephanie L. Budin, *The Myth of Sacred Prostitution in Antiquity* (Cambridge: Cambridge University Press, 2008); Joan Goodnick Westenholz, "Tamar, Qĕdēšā, Qadištu, and Sacred Prostitution in Mesopotamia," *HTR* 82, no. 3 (1989): 245–65; Karel van der Toorn, "Female Prostitution in Payment of Vows in Ancient Israel," *JBL* 108 (1989): 193–205; and Grace I. Emmerson, "Women in Ancient Israel," in *The World of Ancient Israel: Sociological, Anthropological, and Political Perspectives*, ed. R. E. Clements (Cambridge: Cambridge University Press, 1989), 371–94.

39 Hennie Marsman, *Women in Ugarit and Israel: Their Social and Religious Position in the Context of the Ancient Near East* (Atlanta: Society of Biblical Literature, 2003), 497–99. Regarding prostitution in general, Marsman notes that disapproval of this practice is expressed in the book of Leviticus. This prohibition was intended to prevent any uncertainty in the parentage of priestly offspring (*Women in Ugarit*, 434–35). For example, an Israelite father should not degrade his daughter by making her a prostitute (Lev 19:29), and a priest was forbidden to marry a prostitute (Lev 21:7, 14).

40 Beatrice Allard Brooks, "Fertility Cult Functionaries in the Old Testament," *JBL* 60, no. 3 (1941): 239. Though beyond the scope of this chapter, the historical reality of sacred prostitution is highly contested within scholarship. In addition to Brooks, see Karin Adams, "Metaphor and Dissonance: A Reinterpretation of Hosea 4:13-14," *JBL* 127, no. 2 (2008): 291–305; Budin, *Myth of Sacred Prostitution*; and James E. Miller, "A Critical Response to Karin Adams's Reinterpretation of Hosea 4:13-14," *JBL* 128, no. 3 (2009): 503–6.

41 Hamley, "What's Wrong," 43. In her treatment of *zonah* in the Hebrew Bible, Hamley highlights the material found in the books of Jeremiah, Ezekiel, and Hosea.

42 Budin, *Myth of Sacred Prostitution*, 22–23.

43 Martin Gruber suggests the idea of a cultic or sacred prostitute spread like a computer virus that was copied from book to book. See Martin I. Gruber, "Prostitutes and Prostitution in the Bible," *Zmanim: A Historical Quarterly* 90 (2005): 22–29.

44 When the biblical writers discuss male prostitutes, they use the noun *kelev* instead of *zonah*. Although usually translated "dog," the Hebrew *kelev* is the word used to mark a male prostitute in Deut 23:18 (23:19 in Hebrew). Like *zonah*, when used figuratively, *kelev* refers to males who are held in contempt. The term is an insult used to condescendingly describe enemies or useless individuals as in 1 Sam 17:43; 2 Sam 9:8; Ps 22:16; Isa 56:10-11.

# Chapter 2

1 Isabelle Hamley, "What's Wrong with 'Playing the Harlot'? The Meaning of זנה in Judges 19:2," *TynBul* 66, no. 1 (2015): 43.

2 "זָנָה זוֹנָה," *HALOT* 1:275.

3 Phyllis A. Bird, "The Harlot as Heroine: Narrative Art and Social Presupposition in Three Old Testament Texts," *Semeia* 46 (1989): 119–20.

4 For examples, see Marcella Maria Althaus-Reid, "Searching for a Queer Sophia-Wisdom: The Post-Colonial Rahab," in *Patriarchs and Other Villains*, ed. Lisa Isherwood (London: Equinox, 2007), 128–40; Musa W. Dube, "Rahab Is Hanging Out a Red Ribbon: One African Woman's Perspective on the Future of Feminist New Testament Scholarship," in *Feminist New Testament Studies: Global and Future Perspectives*, ed. Kathleen O'Brien Wicker, Althea Spencer Miller, and Musa W. Dube (New York: Palgrave Macmillan, 2005); Kah-Jin Jeffrey Kuan and Mai-Anh Le Tran, "Reading Race Reading Rahab: A 'Broad' Asian American Reading of a 'Broad' Other," in *Postcolonial Interventions: Chapters in Honour of R. S. Sugirtharajah*, ed. Tat-Siong Benny Liew and Rasiah S. Sugirtharajah (Sheffield, UK: Sheffield Phoenix Press, 2009), 27–44; Judith McKinlay, "Rahab: A Hero/ine," *BibInt* 7 (1999); and Suzanne Scholz, "Convert, Prostitute, or Traitor? Rahab as the Anti-Matriarch in Contemporary Biblical Interpretations," in *In the Arms of Biblical Women*, ed. J. T. Greene and M. M. Caspi (Piscataway, NJ: Gorgias, 2013), 147.

5 "קדשׁ," *BDB*, 873. Bernard P. Robinson, "Rahab of Canaan—and Israel," *Scandinavian Journal of the Old Testament* 23, no. 2 (2009): 265.

6 Stephanie L. Budin, *The Myth of Sacred Prostitution in Antiquity* (Cambridge: Cambridge University Press, 2008), 1. Budin offers a definition of sacred prostitution that includes the sale of a person's body for sexual purposes, wherein a portion of the financial proceeds belongs to a deity like the ancient Near Eastern Ištar or Aštarte, or the Greek Aphrodite, and then asserts that her definition is more precisely a sketch of the compilation of many ideas that have emerged over the centuries to finally meld into an image of some sort of a ritual or institution or practice that has been branded and misnamed "sacred prostitution" (3). Daniel

Arnaud, Julia Assante, Everett Ferguson, Stephen Hooks, and Gerter Lerner also contribute to the sacred prostitution conversation.

7   Budin, *Myth of Sacred Prostitution*, 5. Although *BDB* translates *qadeš* (masc.) and *qadeša* (fem.) as "temple prostitute," and the words' association with holiness (the Semitic *qdš* refers to something set apart as in consecration) suggests these individuals would be some type of cult functionaries, there is no material evidence that their function was sexual (33). Furthermore, Budin argues convincingly that the parallel construction of *qedešîm* and *qedešôt* in Deut 23 suggests the biblical writer understood the two titles as a "matched set" such that there is no reason to define a *qadeša* as a prostitute (secular or sacred), but simply as a female cult functionary or as a priestess, as is the case with the male (34).

8   Budin, 8. Although the Italian regions of Pyrgi and Rapino are associated with sacred prostitution, in the absence of literary witnesses, this idea only emerged through circular reasoning and wish-fulfillment. Although the Rapino Bronze inscription concerned revenue derived from the sale of leftover meat used in religious rituals, A. La Regina proposed an alternative interpretation in which he substituted "meat" with "slave girls," whom he identified as sacred prostitutes. In this way, La Regina suggested that the inscription pertains to sacred prostitution, despite the word for sacred prostitution, *ancillae,* not even being in the text. This word was inserted by La Regina on the speculation that the inscription was a reference to an institution his (mis)readings of other documents created (Budin, 247, 258).

9   Martin I. Gruber, "Prostitutes and Prostitution in the Bible," *Zmanim: A Historical Quarterly* 90 (2005): 29.

10  McKinlay, "Rahab: A Hero/ine," 44.

11  McKinlay, 45. Despite no mention of payment for prostitution services in the text, McKinlay expands upon the transactional nature of prostitution when she notes that the paid taking of women is connected to the taking of the land.

12  D. J. Wiseman, "Rahab of Jericho," *TynBul* 14 (1964): 8. Also see *Laws of Hammurabi § 109*.

13  Siduri appears in Tablet X of the Babylonian tale.

14  In ancient Near Eastern law, the innkeeper's failure to report the presence of dissident elements was punishable by death. See *Laws of Hammurabi* § 109.

15  Steed Vernyl Davidson, "Gazing (at) Native Women: Rahab and Jael in Imperializing and Postcolonial Discourses," in *Postcolonialism and the Hebrew Bible: The Next Step*, ed. Roland Boer (Atlanta: Society of Biblical Literature, 2013), 72. Davidson is careful to use "postcolonial" to denote "the need to move beyond and think beyond the experiences of colonialism while retaining the resistant character of the anti-imperializing moment."

16  Davidson, "Native Women," 73. See Lori Rowlett, "Disney's Pocahontas and Joshua's Rahab in Postcolonial Perspective," in *Culture, Entertainment and the Bible,* ed. George Aichele (Sheffield, UK: Sheffield Academic Press, 2000), 68.

17 Davidson, "Native Women," 76. See Berel Dov Lerner, "Rahab the Harlot and Other Philosophers of Religion," *JBQ* 28 (2000), 52; and Robinson, "Rahab of Canaan," 257.

18 Aaron Sherwood, "A Leader's Misleading and a Prostitute's Profession: A Re-Examination of Joshua 2," *JSOT* 31, no. 1 (2006): 48.

19 See Sherwood, "A Leader's Misleading," 52.

20 "בוא‎," *BDB*, 97; "שָׁכַב‎," *BDB*, 1011; and "יָדַע‎," *BDB*, 393. These terms commonly function as euphemisms for sexual activity. Sherwood, "A Leader's Misleading," 50.

21 Sherwood, 52.

# Chapter 3

1 Howard Thurman, *Jesus and the Disinherited* (Boston: Beacon, 1996), 30.

2 Scholars have also taken up issues such as Rahab's appearance in classical literature like Dante's *Paradise*. See Peter S. Hawkins, "Dante's Rahab," *MLN* 124, no. 5 (2009): S70–S80.

3 Phyllis A. Bird, "The Harlot as Heroine: Narrative Art and Social Presupposition in Three Old Testament Texts," *Semeia* 46 (1989): 119–39. Also, Phyllis Silverman Kramer argues that the stories of Tamar, who disguised herself as a harlot in Gen 38; the two postpartum prostitute mothers who require King Solomon to adjudicate their claim to a child in 1 Kgs 3; and Rahab of Josh 2 each require as their presupposition a view of the harlot as a marginal figure in the society. See Kramer, "Rahab: From Peshat to Pedagogy, or: The Many Faces of a Heroine," in *Culture, Entertainment and the Bible,* ed. George Aichele (Sheffield, UK: Sheffield Academic Press, 2000), 156–73.

4 Bird, "Harlot as Heroine," 129. Moreover, Rahab's story turns on the axis of the irony of a harlot becoming a hero. The layered construction of the narrative invites the reader to speculate about Rahab's possible motives. Bird suggests that Rahab's decision to assist the spies may be a response to hostility felt toward the king and his affiliates, a matter of self-interest (if the enemy spies are found on her premises she will be penalized), or a class-driven decision by which the social outcast among her own people aligns with the representatives of an outcast people on the move who may offer her a new—better—future.

5 Aaron Sherwood, "A Leader's Misleading and a Prostitute's Profession: A Re-Examination of Joshua 2," *JSOT* 31, no. 1 (2006): 47. Sherwood highlights how this story's intertextuality with other spying accounts and Gen 19, the negative language by which the Israelites' spying becomes their pursuit, and innuendo regarding sexuality work together to encourage the reader to expect disaster will fall upon the spies and that Joshua's mission will end in failure. But Rahab's heroic diversion tactics result in the spies averting calamity (52).

6 Rahab's superhero status is all the more compelling because, as Sherwood points out, whereas prostitution is a Deuteronomic metaphor for idolatrous apostasy, Rahab's profession strengthens her identity as a Canaanite and underscores the

Canaanites' threatening practice of "whoring after idols." In this way the narrator sets the reader up to expect nothing positive from Rahab (Sherwood, "Leader's Misleading," 48).

7   After Shechem sexually violates Dinah, *zonah* is the word used when her brothers confront him for treating their sister "like a whore." In Rahab's story and the story of Tamar in Gen 38, *zonah* describes one who participates in an activity in which there is some sort of sexual exchange, a rape, or proof of sexual intercourse in the form of a pregnancy. In Proverbs, the sexualized imagery of *zonah* carries negative connotations. The didactic "teacher" of Proverbs speaks of "a prostitute's fee" (Prov 6:26), identifies someone as dressing "like a prostitute" (7:10), warns that "a prostitute is a deep pit" (23:27), and admonishes the student that "to keep company with prostitutes is to squander one's substance" (29:3).

8   Athalya Brenner-Idan, *The Israelite Woman: Social Role and Literary Type in Biblical Narrative* (Sheffield, UK: JSOT Press, 1985), 80.

9   This is also the case in the stories of Dinah in Gen 34 and Tamar in Gen 38.

10   The writer of Judg 11:1 leads readers to believe the father could be any man from Gilead.

11   See Randall C. Bailey, "He Didn't Even Tell Us the Worst of It!," *USQR* 59, no. 1 (2005): 15–24; Bradley L. Crowell, "Good Girl, Bad Girl: Foreign Women of the Deuteronomistic History in Postcolonial Perspective," *BibInt* 21, no. 1 (2013): 1–18; and Bird, "Harlot as Heroine."

12   Bailey, "Worst of It!," 20. Bailey also maps out this destabilization strategy in "They're Nothing but Incestuous Bastards: The Polemical Use of Sex and Sexuality in Hebrew Canon Narratives," in *Reading from This Place: Social Location and Biblical Interpretation in the United States*, vol. 1 (Minneapolis: Fortress, 1995), 131–38.

13   Crowell, "Good Girl, Bad Girl," 6. Crowell is interested in demonstrating how foreign women are described in hypersexualized terms in both the Deuteronomistic History and the colonial/postcolonial literature. His article exposes how foreign women are constructed as symbolic of the threat of cultural hybridity. Crowell points out that, as a foreign woman defined only by her occupation as a prostitute, but one who displays her loyalty to both Yahweh and the invading Israelites, Rahab is ambiguous (7).

14   See Eccl. Rabbah 8:10:1; Num. Rabbah 16:1; Larry L. Lyke, "What Does Ruth Have to Do with Rahab? Midrash Ruth Rabbah and the Matthean Genealogy of Jesus," in *The Function of Scripture in Early Jewish and Christian Tradition*, ed. Craig A. Evans and James A. Sanders, JSOTSup 154 (Sheffield, UK: Sheffield Academic Press, 1998), 262–84; and Byron L. Sherwin, "Heinous Sin: Harbinger of Catastrophe or Redemption?" *JBQ* 40, no. 2 (2012): 81–88.

15   Ira D. Mangililo, "When Rahab and Indonesian Christian Women Meet in the Third Space," *JFSR* 31, no. 1 (2015): 45–64.

16   Athalya Brenner, *I Am . . . : Biblical Women Tell Their Own Stories* (Minneapolis: Fortress, 2004).

17  See Charles B. Copher, "The Black Presence in the Old Testament," in *Stony the Road We Trod: African American Biblical Interpretation,* ed. Cain Hope Felder (Minneapolis: Fortress, 1991), 146–64; Copher, *Black Biblical Studies: Biblical and Theological Issues on the Black Presence in the Bible: An Anthology of Charles B. Copher* (Chicago: Black Light Fellowship, 1993); and Copher, "Blacks/Negroes: Participants in the Development of Civilization in the Ancient World and Their Presence in the Bible," *Journal of the Interdenominational Theological Center* 23, no. 1 (1995): 3–47. While Daniel Hawk has examined identity in the book of Joshua, his concern is the formation of group/community identity for the Israelites. See L. Daniel Hawk, "Fixing Boundaries: The Construction of Identity in Joshua," *Ashland Theological Journal* 32 (2000): 21–31.

18  George M. Fredrickson, *The Arrogance of Race: Historical Perspectives on Slavery, Racism, and Social Inequality* (Middletown, CT: Wesleyan University Press, 1988), 237.

19  Gunner Myrdal, Richard Sterner, and Arnold Rose, *An American Dilemma: The Negro Problem and Modern Democracy* (New York: Harper and Row, 1962), 683.

20  Elaine K. Ginsberg, ed., *Passing and the Fictions of Identity* (Durham: Duke University Press, 1996), 64. In 1859 a Philadelphia newspaper reported the story of Sam, a "bright mulatto" who reportedly could "scarcely be distinguished from a white man." Sam's slave trader, "Black Matt," dressed him in fine clothes, a silk hat, and kid gloves, and encouraged Sam to show himself off. As the story goes, in a sudden reversal of fortune, Sam sold Black Matt into slavery, boarded a ship headed for a European port, and was never seen again.

21  Allyson Hobbs, *A Chosen Exile: A History of Racial Passing in American Life* (Cambridge: Harvard University Press, 2014), 28–29.

22  William Still, *The Underground Railroad: A Record of Facts, Authentic Narratives, Letters, Etc. Narrating the Hardships, Hairbreadth Escapes and Death Struggles of the Slaves in Their Efforts for Freedom, as Related by Themselves and Others, or Witnessed by the Author; Together with Sketches of Some of the Largest Stockholders, and Most Liberal Aiders and Advisors of the Road* (1871; repr. Chicago: Johnson, 1970), 218–19.

23  Martha J. Cutter, "Sliding Significations: Passing as a Narrative and Textual Strategy in Nella Larsen's Fiction," in Ginsberg, *Passing and the Fictions of Identity,* 73.

24  Nella Larsen, *The Complete Fiction of Nella Larsen: "Passing," "Quicksand," and "The Stories,"* ed. Charles R. Larson (New York: Anchor Books, 2001), 74.

25  Cutter, "Sliding Significations," 79.

26  Larsen, *Complete Fiction of Nella Larsen,* xiv; and Cutter, "Sliding Significations," 81.

27  Larsen, 181.

28  Larsen, 181.

29  Perhaps the most direct threat to Clare's passing is the existence of offspring. As the grandchildren of a Black man, Clare's children pose a threat to her passing if

they possess phonotypical traits typically associated with Black people, such as dark skin and coarse hair. Conveniently, readers are told that Clare's mixed-race daughter Margery is light skinned, but Margery (and the danger she presents if hue betrays her) is literally stashed away from Clare's community of choice because she is attending school in Switzerland.

30 The Hebrew verb *shkhv* translates as "lie" and, like the verb *yda* ("to know"), is a euphemism for sexual intercourse. In addition to basic verbs meaning "lie," "love," "know," "come," and "enter," a great many euphemisms relate to sex, especially sexual body parts. For more on euphemisms in the biblical text see Scott B. Noegel, "Euphemism in the Hebrew Bible," in *Encyclopedia of Hebrew Language and Linguistics,* ed. Geoffrey Khan, vol. 1 (Leiden: Brill, 2013), 869–71; Shalom M. Paul, "The Shared Legacy of Sexual Metaphors and Euphemisms," in *Sex and Gender in the Ancient Near East: Proceedings of the 47th Rencontre Assyriologique Internationale Helsinki, July 2-6, 2001,* ed. Simo Parpola and Robert M. Whiting (Helsinki: Neo-Assyrian Text Corpus Project, 2002), 489–98; Joseph Epstein, "Sex and Euphemism," *Commentary* 77, no. 4 (Apr. 1984): 55–60; and Sandie Gravett, "Reading 'Rape' in the Hebrew Bible: A Consideration of Language," *JSOT* 28, no. 3 (Mar. 2004): 279–99.

31 Hobbs, *Chosen Exile,* 159.

# Chapter 4

1 The character Salmon is mentioned as Salma in 1 Chr 2:11. For information on this variant spelling see Kirk E. Lowery, "Salmon (Person)," *ABD* 5:906.

2 The "whore with a heart of gold" or "hooker with a heart of gold" character, made popular in literature, opera, and cinema by Sonya Semyonovna Marmeladova in Fyodor Dostoevsky's novel *Crime and Punishment,* Violetta Valery in Giuseppe Verdi's opera *La Traviata,* and Julia Roberts's Vivian Ward in the movie *Pretty Woman,* is a (reluctant) sex worker who demonstrates integrity and a moral center while dispensing advice or acting as a go-between for other characters in the piece. See T. J. Wray, *Good Girls, Bad Girls: The Enduring Lessons of Twelve Women of the Old Testament* (Lanham, MD: Rowman & Littlefield, 2008).

3 For discussion on the treatment of women captured in war in the biblical text and ancient societies see A. Brenner, *A Feminist Companion to the Latter Prophets* (Sheffield, UK: Sheffield Academic Press, 1995); C. Pressler, *The View of Women Found in the Deuteronomic Family Laws* (Berlin: De Gruyter, 2014); S. B. Thistlethwaite, "'You May Enjoy the Spoil of Your Enemies': Rape as a Biblical Metaphor for War," *Semeia* 61 (1993): 59–75; I. J. Gelb, "Prisoners of War in Early Mesopotamia," *JNES* 32 (1973): 70–98; and H. I. Avalos, "The Ancient Near Eastern and Biblical Roots of Human Trafficking by ISIS," *Conversations with the Biblical World* 36 (2016): 199–224.

4 Phyllis Trible, *Rhetorical Criticism: Context, Method, and the Book of Jonah* (Minneapolis: Fortress, 1994), 8. Trible restates the five canons or tenets of rhetoric originally articulated by the Roman philosopher Cicero in *De Inventione.*

5 The Hexateuch is the first six books of the Bible.

6 "Chiasm," *Pocket Dictionary for the Study of New Testament Greek* (Downers Grove, IL: IVP Academic, 2001), 29. Also, Allen P. Ross, *Introducing Biblical Hebrew,* Accordance electronic ed. (Grand Rapids: Baker Books, 2001), paragraph 6832. For more information on chiasmus see Nils Wilhelm Lund, "The Presence of Chiasmus in the Old Testament," *The American Journal of Semitic Languages and Literatures* 46, no. 2 (1930): 104–26.

7 For discussions of Canaan as the promised land see Irvine H. Anderson, *Biblical Interpretation and Middle East Policy: The Promised Land, America, and Israel, 1917-2002* (Gainesville: University Press of Florida, 2005); B. Tarkington, *The Conquest of Canaan* (Charlottesville: University of Virginia Library, 1995); Ronald S. Hendel, *The Epic of the Patriarch: The Joseph Cycle and the Narrative Traditions of Canaan and Israel* (Atlanta: Scholars Press, 1987); and Nili Wazana, *All the Boundaries of the Land: The Promised Land in Biblical Thought in Light of the Ancient Near East* (University Park, PA: Eisenbrauns, 2013).

8 Trible, *Rhetorical Criticism*, 8. Also see James Muilenburg, "A Study in Hebrew Rhetoric: Repetition and Style," *VTSup* 1 (Leiden: Brill, 1953), 97–111.

9 Again, יצא (*ytza*) appears in the Hiphil imperative in the Genesis and Joshua narratives.

10 Andrzej Toczyski, *The 'Geometrics' of the Rahab Story: A Multi-dimensional Analysis of Joshua 2* (New York: T & T Clark, 2018).

11 Toczyski, *'Geometrics,'* 104. Toczyski points to Siegfried Wagner's six elements belonging to the genre called the "spy narrative." Some scholars, like Gene M. Tucker and Dennis J. McCarthy, reject elements of Wagner's application of the schema to Rahab's story. See Tucker, "The Rahab Saga (Joshua 2): Some Form-Critical and Tradition-Historical Observations," in *The Use of the Old Testament in the New and Other Chapters: Studies in Honor of William Franklin Stinespring,* ed. J. M. Efird (Durham: Duke University Press, 1972), 66–86; and McCarthy, "The Theology of Leadership in Joshua 1-9," *Bib* 52 (1971): 165–75.

12 The writer uses the Hebrew verb נצל (*ntzl*) in Josh 2:13. *Ntzl* is the same verb used to describe the LORD's act of freeing the Israelites from Egypt throughout Exodus (for instance, 5:23; 6:6; 12:36; 18:4, 8; 33:6).

13 Rahab is the mother of Boaz, the grandmother of Obed, and the great-grandmother of Jesse, the father of King David. See Ruth 4:16-22; Matt 1:3-6; and Luke 3:32.

14 Randall C. Bailey, "They're Nothing but Incestuous Bastards: The Polemical Use of Sex and Sexuality in Hebrew Canon Narratives," in *Reading from This Place: Social Location and Biblical Interpretation in the United States,* vol. 1 (Minneapolis: Fortress, 1995), 131–38.

15 Randall C. Bailey, "He Didn't Even Tell Us the Worst of It!," *USQR* 59, no. 1 (2005): 15–24. Bailey examines Rahab's story in Josh 2, the story of the Gibeonites who tricked the Israelites into making a treaty with them in Josh 9:3-27, and the story of the people who played a pivotal role in the coalition building of the kings of the South and the North to stop the invasion of their land by the Israelites in Josh 10–11.

16 Bailey, "Worst of It!," 20. Bailey also maps out this destabilization strategy in "They're Nothing but Incestuous Bastards."

17 Bailey, "Worst of It!," 22.

18 Bailey, 23. Also see Danna Nolan Fewell's chapter, "Deconstructive Criticism: Ashsah and the (E)razed City of Writing," in *Judges & Method: New Approaches in Biblical Studies*, ed. Gale A. Yee (Minneapolis: Fortress, 1995), 119–45, for a treatment of the destruction of intellectual property.

19 I have used NRSV here, but similar wording exists in NIV, JPS, and CEB in which the Israelite men express concern about others learning of their mission.

20 The Hebrew noun *debir* may be translated "speech," "word," or "matter (i.e., business, occupation)." "דָּבָר," *BDB*, 182.

21 That many Bible dictionaries list "Treaty, see Covenant, Covenants" is instructive. This lexical classification suggests treaties and covenants are synonymous.

22 See 1 Sam 11:1-2, 1 Kgs 5:12, Hos 12:1, and Josh 9:6-16. In all of these cases the text uses the Hebrew formula *krt berit* (translation, "cut or make a covenant") to describe the treaty-making process. Within the worldview of the ancient Israelites, a treaty was the same as a covenant. The Hebrew term for covenant, *berit*, denotes political agreements between individuals, between kings (as representatives of prescribed regions), or between kings and individuals. The biblical writers chronicle covenants between individuals such as Abraham and Abimelech (Gen 21:27) and between kings like Solomon and Hiram (1 Kings 5:12) or the king of Judah and Nebuchadnezzar (Ezek 17:13).

23 The Hebrew phrase "to cut a covenant" points to the idea that the ancients conceptualized treaty and covenant similarly.

24 Interpreters like René Lopez and John Thompson address this issue. See René Lopez, "Israelite Covenants in the Light of Ancient Near Eastern Covenants," *Chafer Theological Seminary Journal* 9, no. 2 (2003): 92–111; and John A. Thompson, "The Significance of the Ancient Near Eastern Treaty Pattern," *TynBul* 13, no. 2 (1963).

25 K. M. Campbell suggests the stipulations are the protections promised to the house of Rahab on the condition of obedience in vv. 12-13 and 18-20 ("Rahab's Covenant: A Short Note on Joshua ii 9-21," *VT* 22, no. 2 [1972]: 243).

26 Campbell, "Rahab's Covenant," 243. The two spies' declaration, "Our lives for yours," may also be considered the asking for a sign.

27 Max Weber, *Economy and Society: An Outline of Interpretive Sociology* (Berkeley: University of California Press, 1978), 53. Weber conceptualizes power as "*power-over*." Also see Robert Dahl, "The Concept of Power," *Behavioral Science* 2 (1957): 201–15, for a treatment of *power-over*, which Dahl frames as the "intuitive idea of power." See also Hanna Fenichel Pitkin, *Wittgenstein and Justice: On the Significance of Ludwig Wittgenstein for Social and Political Thought* (Berkeley: University of California Press, 1972); Thomas Hobbes, *Leviathan*; and Mark Haugaard, "Power: A 'Family Resemblance' Concept," *European Journal of Cultural Studies* 13 (2010): 419–38, for discussions of power as an ability or capacity.

28 Kimberly D. Russaw, *Daughters in the Hebrew Bible* (Lanham, MD: Lexington Books/Fortress Academic, 2018), 106.

29 Campbell, "Rahab's Covenant," 243–44. Also see D. J. Wiseman, "Rahab of Jericho," *TynBul* 14 (1964): 8–11.

30 See Reinhard Achenbach, Rainer Albertz, and Jakob Wöhrle, eds., *The Foreigner and the Law: Perspectives from the Hebrew Bible and the Ancient Near East* (Atlanta: SBL Press, 2011); Noel Weeks, *Admonition and Curse: The Ancient Near Eastern Treaty/Covenant Form as a Problem in Inter-Cultural Relationships* (New York: T & T Clark, 2004); René Lopez, "Israelite Covenants"; and John A. Thompson, "Ancient Near Eastern Treaty Pattern."

31 Scholars acknowledge three major theories of how the Israelites settled in Canaan. William Albright articulated the Conquest Model, which comports with the Joshua narrative. Albrecht Alt represents those scholars who advance the Peaceful Infiltration Model, which understands the Israelites' evolution from a nomadic to a sedentary life over time, a process that resulted in them settling in Canaan. Norman Gottwald and George Mendenhall represent those scholars who support the Peasant Revolt Model, in which disgruntled citizens of Canaan helped the Israelites conquer urban centers.

# Chapter 5

1 Randall C. Bailey, "He Didn't Even Tell Us the Worst of It!," *USQR* 59, no. 1 (2005): 20.

2 Rahab does not reappear until the New Testament, in Matthew.

3 Ruth 4:21 and 1 Chr 2:11 identify Salmon (Salma and Sala are variant spellings) as the father of Boaz and the great-great-grandfather of King David. It is only with Matt 1:5 that we are told Rahab was thought to be the partner or wife of Salmon. See Kirk E. Lowery, "Salmon (Person)," *ABD* 5:906.

4 The scholarship does not always align with the biblical account of the conquest narrative. In Albrecht Alt's Peaceful Infiltration Model, for example, the Israelite immigrants were nomadic or seminomadic peoples who arrived over an extended period of time. These semi-nomadic Israelites encountered Canaanites time and time again. That the Canaanites remained in the land—as seen in various portions of the Book of Judges—challenges the Conquest Model and undergirds the scholarly inquiry of Alt and others. Additionally, George Mendenhall introduced the Peasant Revolt Model, which asserts that the Israelites' entry into Canaan was all an "inside job." Mendenhall sees most of the conquerors as of indigenous—that is, Canaanite—origin. As the theory goes, peasant farmers grew tired of urban overlords so they revolted. Importantly, the catalysts for the revolt were a "group of slave-labor captives who had succeeded in escaping an intolerable situation in Egypt" and had "established a relationship with a deity, YHWH." Notably, these three theories (some scholars suggest there are five theories of settlement) all have their challenges. For more information on theories of the Israelites' entry into Canaan see Albrecht Alt, *Essays on Old Testament History and Religion*, trans. R. A. Wilson (Garden City, NY: Doubleday, 1968); John Bright,

*A History of Israel* (Louisville: Westminster John Knox, 2000); Michael D. Coogan, "Archaeology and Biblical Studies: The Book of Joshua," in *The Hebrew Bible and Its Interpreters,* ed. W.H. Propp, B. Halpern, and D. N. Freedman (Winona Lake, IN: Eisenbrauns, 1990), 19–30; and G. E. Mendenhall, "The Hebrew Conquest of Palestine," *BA* 25 (1962): 66–87.

5 For more information on *herem*, see J. P. U. Lilley, "Understanding the Herem," *TynBul* 44, no. 1 (May 1993), pp. 169–77.

6 While I am aware the text has been shaped over time and contains anachronistic themes and concerns, in this project I accept the text in its final form and have little concern for matters of dating, redaction, or emendation. Importantly, in this chapter, I am not concerned with extra-biblical material such as rabbinic references that attempt to read beyond the biblical text.

7 Julie Galambush proposes the "genocide" texts may work as a tool assuring the Israelite returnees from the Babylonian exile that they are YHWH's chosen people, entering the land under divine mandate. Galambush also acknowledges the dichotomous relationship between the two major commandments Israel receives regarding how they are to enter and live in the land. One is a mandate to champion the rights of the oppressed "other," and the second is a mandate to eliminate the other in the name of God. For Galambush, the scenario of the two sets of commandments being sequential (the Israelites first slaughter all non-Israelites, then occupy the land and welcome the non-Israelites wishing to live there subsequently) makes little sense for contemporary readers. Julie Galambush, "Be Kind to Strangers, But Kill the Canaanites: A Feminist Biblical Theology of the Other," in *After Exegesis: Feminist Biblical Theology: Chapters in Honor of Carol A. Newsom,* ed. Patricia K. Tull and Jacqueline E. Lapsley (Waco: Baylor University Press, 2015), 141–48.

8 The inability of the Ephraimites to drive out the Canaanites is also found in Judg 1:29.

9 I. J. Gelb, "Prisoners of War in Early Mesopotamia," *JNES* 32 (1973): 90. Although Gelb points to no tangible evidence that POWs were distributed to individuals such as generals or nobles, he suggests such practices were followed in early Mesopotamian times, as they were throughout ancient history (81).

10 The Israelites fought against Amalek (Exod 17), the Canaanites and the Amorites (Num 21), the Midianites (Num 31), Jericho (Josh 6), Ai (Josh 7–8), and various kings and cities in North and South Palestine (Josh 10–11).

11 Deborah, Barak, and Jael led the fight against the Canaanites (Judg 4); Gideon fought the Midianites (Judg 7); Jephthah made his famous vow while in battle against the Ammonites (Judg 11); and both Eli and Samuel waged war against the Philistines (1 Sam 4 and 7).

12 King David fought Abner (2 Sam 2–3) and Absalom (2 Sam 15–18).

13 "Booty," *The New International Dictionary of the Bible* (Grand Rapids: Zondervan, 1999), 170.

14 S. B. Thistlethwaite, "'You May Enjoy the Spoil of Your Enemies': Rape as a Biblical Metaphor for War," *Semeia* 61 (1993): 66.

15 Gerhard von Rad, *Old Testament Theology* (Edinburgh: Oliver and Boyd, 1962), 307. Thistlethwaite notes the "supreme leader of armies" expression appears more than two hundred times in the biblical text ("Spoil of Your Enemies," 67).

16 Phyllis A. Bird, "The Harlot as Heroine: Narrative Art and Social Presupposition in Three Old Testament Texts," *Semeia* 46 (1989): 127.

17 Deuteronomy 7:2 and 19:1 establish that the Israelites are to show no mercy to those enemies whom God gives to them. The Israelites are to annihilate the enemy, dispossess them of their land, and settle in their cities. That the Israelites have not done so is commentary on God's ability to give the enemy into the hand of the Israelites.

18 Gordon J. Wenham, "The Deuteronomic Theology of the Book of Joshua," *JBL* 90, no. 2 (1971): 140–48. Also see Yehezkel Kaufmann, *The Biblical Account of the Conquest of Palestine* (Jerusalem: Hebrew University Press, 1953).

19 Richard Gabriel approaches this recognition when he reminds his readers the entire book of Joshua is a saga of *military* conquest. Gabriel's introduction of "military" language points to warfare, but he too softens the image with the use of "conquest." Richard A. Gabriel, *The Military History of Ancient Israel* (Westport, CT: Praeger, 2003), 109.

20 Thistlethwaite, "Spoil of Your Enemies," 66.

21 Wenham, "Deuteronomic Theology," 142.

22 Wenham, 141.

23 Wenham, 142.

24 Wenham, 141, 146.

25 Thistlethwaite, "Spoil of Your Enemies," 67. As an example, warriors "offered themselves willingly" in Judg 5:2.

26 Thistlethwaite, 68.

27 Niditch argues Josh 6 reflects broader ancient Near Eastern notions of war as "crusade." Susan Niditch, "War, Women, and Defilement in Numbers 31," *Semeia* 61 (1993): 43.

28 Although they do not always treat Rahab specifically, scholars take up the idea of foreignness or the "other" in ways that have bearing on Rahab's narrative. For example, Saul Olyan examines various rhetorical signifiers used by the biblical writers to stigmatize foreigners, alien objects, and alien practices. Olyan's treatment of abomination, illegitimate profanation of holiness, sin, and the ban (*herem*) may inform readings of Rahab as a foreign woman. Julie Galambush considers why biblical editors included oddly juxtaposed messages for the Israelites to slaughter all of Canaan's residents and protect the rights of all non-Israelites in the commandments found in Deut 20:16-17 and Lev 19:33-34, respectively. Galambush's work prompts questions around the treatment of Rahab and her family after the destruction of Jericho. See Saul M. Olyan, "Stigmatizing Associations:

The Alien, Things Alien, and Practices Associated with Aliens in Biblical Classification Schemas," in *The Foreigner and the Law: Perspectives from the Hebrew Bible and the Ancient Near East*, ed. Reinhard Achenbach, Rainer Albertz, and Jakob Wöhrle (Wiesbaden, Ger.: Harrassowitz, 2011), 17–28; and Julie Galambush, "Be Kind to Strangers," 141–54.

29 Bailey, "Worst of It!," 20.

30 Suzanne Scholz, "Convert, Prostitute, or Traitor? Rahab as the Anti-Matriarch in Contemporary Biblical Interpretations," in *In the Arms of Biblical Women*, ed. J. T. Greene and M. M. Caspi (Piscataway, NJ: Gorgias, 2013), 178. Scholz points to four major trends in Josh 2 exegesis: source-critical interpretations, conservative Christian readings, gynocentric-feminist approaches, and postcolonial feminist, queer, and ethnic readings (149).

31 L. Daniel Hawk, "Indigenous Helpers and Invader Homelands," in *Joshua and Judges*, ed. Athalya Brenner and Gale A. Yee (Minneapolis: Fortress, 2013), 109–22.

32 Gelb, "Prisoners of War in Early Mesopotamia," 95.

33 Gelb, 83–86.

34 Gelb, 81.

35 Stefan Reif, "What Enraged Phinehas: A Study of Numbers 25:8," *JBL* 90, no. 2 (1971): 205.

36 Olyan, "Stigmatizing Associations."

37 Stefan Reif argues that Cozbi (Num 25) may have been brought into the tent of the Israelite Zimri to engage in divination (ostensibly to rid the Israelites of a plague), and Phinehas was offended at the usurpation of his priestly rights and at this further act of apostasy from YHWH. ("What Enraged Phinehas," 205).

# INDEX